UNIVERSITY OF NORTH CAROLINA AT CHAPEL HILL
DEPARTMENT OF ROMANCE LANGUAGES

NORTH CAROLINA STUDIES
IN THE ROMANCE LANGUAGES AND LITERATURES

Founder: URBAN TIGNER HOLMES

Distributed by:

UNIVERSITY OF NORTH CAROLINA PRESS

CHAPEL HILL
North Carolina 27514
U.S.A.

NORTH CAROLINA STUDIES IN THE
ROMANCE LANGUAGES AND LITERATURES
Number 199

LA QUERELLE DE LA ROSE:
LETTERS AND DOCUMENTS

LA QUERELLE DE LA ROSE:

Letters and Documents

BY

JOSEPH L. BAIRD
AND
JOHN R. KANE

CHAPEL HILL

NORTH CAROLINA STUDIES IN THE ROMANCE
LANGUAGES AND LITERATURES
U.N.C. DEPARTMENT OF ROMANCE LANGUAGES
1978

Library of Congress Cataloging in Publication Data

Main entry under title:
La Querelle de la Rose.

(North Carolina studies in the Romance languages and literatures; 199)
Bibliography: p.
1. Roman de la Rose. 2. Women—Social conditions. 3. Women's rights.
I. Baird, Joseph L. II. Kane, John Robert, 1933-   III. Series.

PQ1529.Q43   841'.1   78-14815
ISBN 0-8078-9199-1

I.S.B.N. 0-8078-199-1

PRINTED IN SPAIN

IMPRESO EN ESPAÑA

DEPÓSITO LEGAL: V. 2.241 - 1978   I.S.B.N. 84-399-8748-X
ARTES GRÁFICAS SOLER, S. A. - JÁVEA, 28 - VALENCIA (8) - 1978

ad uxores
sine quibus non

TABLE OF CONTENTS

Page

INTRODUCTION   11

LETTERS AND DOCUMENTS

Christine de Pisan, *L'Epistre au Dieu d'Amours* (Excerpts)   35

Jean de Montreuil, Remarks concerning the Lost Treatise   39

Jean de Montreuil, Letter, *Cum ut dant sese res*   40

Jean de Montreuil, Letter, *Quo magis*   42

Jean de Montreuil, Letter, *Etsi facundissimus*   44

Christine de Pisan, Letter to Jean de Montreuil   46

Gontier Col, Letter to Christine de Pisan   57

Gontier Col, Letter to Christine de Pisan   60

Christine de Pisan, Letter to Gontier Col   62

Christine de Pisan, Letter to the Queen   65

Christine de Pisan, Letter to Guillaume de Tignonville   67

Christine's Explanation   68

Jean Gerson, *Traité against the Roman de la Rose*   70

Pierre Col, Letter to Christine de Pisan   92

Christine de Pisan, Letter to Pierre Col   116

Jean Gerson, Letter to Pierre Col   145

Jean de Montreuil, Letter, *Ut sunt mores*   153

Jean de Montreuil, Letter, *Ex quo nuge*   156

Jean Gerson, Sermon, *Poenitemini: Par le merveilleux*   158

Pierre Col, Letter to Christine de Pisan (Fragment)   160

Jean Gerson, Sermon, *Poenitemini: En benoiste journee*   162

Jean de Montreuil, Letter, *Scis me*   165

Jean Gerson, Sermon, *Poenitemini: Bien a point et appropos* ...   168

BIBLIOGRAPHY   169

INTRODUCTION

in eas litteras mortuos quasi vivos invenimus

The early fifteenth-century debate on the *Roman de la Rose* began at the very opening of the century, in 1400 or 1401, and continued sporadically and intermittently for a period of approximately two years. This *débat littéraire* originated apparently — we have it on Christine's authority — in what appear to have been informal literary discussions between Christine de Pisan and Jean de Montreuil. There may, in fact, have been at least one other person involved in these early discussions, although the MSS. clearly specify only Montreuil and Christine, because, as the MSS. also tell us, Montreuil sent his now-lost treatise not only to Christine but also to a certain "notable clerc." [1] It would be possible to argue for an even earlier date for the origin of the debate, since in 1399 Christine de Pisan attacked Jean de Meun harshly in *L'Epistre au Dieu d'Amours,* and this attack could, in fact, have led to the discussions. At all events, the *débat* proper begins, as Christine sees it, with these discussions, which led in turn to a formal, structured, and more or less firmly interlinked series of letters (along with one rather more loosely connected treatise) debating the worth, in moral terms, of the *Roman de la Rose.* This controversy, however, should not be viewed merely as a kind of lofty exchange of views among a small group of the sophisticated, albeit rather moralistic, *litterati* of the time. The evidence seems to indicate that the debate was quite a live issue of real and earnest moral interest to a large

---

[1] See Charles Frederick Ward, *The Epistles on the Romance of the Rose and Other Documents in the Debate* (Chicago, 1911), p. 36. See also page 68 of this volume.

number of people. The fact that the notable Jean Gerson addressed himself to the subject in a series of sermons is, in this regard, most significant. Unlike some of Gerson's work delivered in Latin to a specialized and learned audience, these sermons were preached to the populace in the vernacular and thus apparently indicate a widespread interest in the debate. All such writings and orations — Gerson's sermons have come down to us in manuscript — are generally summed up by the title *La Querelle de la Rose,* sometimes viewed as a first phase in that later, more voluminous *débat* of the sixteenth century, *La Querelle des Femmes.* The principals in the *Querelle de la Rose* were some of the most important personages of their day. The defenders of the *Rose* numbered among their ranks Jean de Montreuil, Provost of Lille and sometime Secretary to the Dukes of Berry, Burgundy, and Orleans; to the Dauphin; and to Charles VI, King of France; Gontier Col, First Secretary and Notary to the King; and his brother, Pierre Col, Canon of Paris and Tournay. On the other side, besides Christine — notable, among her contemporaries, mainly because she was an articulate female, "for the novelty of the thing," as Christine herself says in a slightly different context — there was Jean Gerson, famous Chancellor of the University of Paris and, by any standard, one of the most notable men of his time. These are the people for whom we have documents. Some documents, of course, may, like Montreuil's Treatise, have been lost. It is a noteworthy fact, for example, that Christine can feel confident enough to send a collection of the documents, accompanying a request for aid to Guillaume de Tignonville, the eminent provost of Paris, and to Queen Isabeau herself. [2]

Since A. Piaget's important article, "Chronologie des Epistres sur le Roman de la Rose," [3] the dating and chronology of the doc-

---

[2] No letters of support from either Tignonville or the Queen have come down to us. Blanche Hinman Dow, however, believes that the "lettre" Christine receives at the end of *Le Dit de la Rose* is a veiled allusion to a letter of support from Queen Isabeau. See *The Varying Attitude toward Women in French Literature of the Fifteenth Century: The Opening Years* (New York: Publications of the Institute of French Studies, Inc., 1936), p. 189.

[3] In *Etudes romanes dédiées à Gaston Paris* (Paris: Bouillon, 1891), pp. 113-120. Piaget points out, among other matters, that MS. Bibl. nat. fr. 604 incorrectly gives *mil cccc et vii* at the end of Gontier Col's letter to Christine

uments in the debate, aside from the intractable problem of Montreuil's letters, have been well established. Montreuil poses the greatest problems in the historical reconstruction of the debate: not only is his treatise, the first document in the quarrel, now lost, but his other letters lack both date and addressee. The problems involved in these letters, as well as the general chronological scheme for the entire debate, including Gerson's sermons, have been handled most recently and most convincingly by Peter Potansky.[4] The chronology adopted herein, therefore, with one exception, is that suggested by Potansky. The one exception is Christine's reply to Pierre Col. All scholars who have concerned themselves with the Quarrel have, for one reason or another, dated Gerson's answer to Pierre Col earlier than Christine's.[5] Yet this seems hardly likely. It is true, to be sure, that Gerson speaks of having received Col's letter "yesterday" (*hesterno*),[6] but it is not altogether clear, as Potansky points out in another connection (p. 128), whether he received it from Pierre Col himself or from Christine — the letter, after all, was addressed only to Christine. It seems clear, at all events, that Gerson has read not only Col's letter but also Christine's reply. At one point, for example, Gerson writes:

> Then this lady [he is speaking of Christine, whom he has named specifically in the preceding sentences] shrewdly pointed out that not only queens but also any right-minded person endowed with natural modesty would blush at a reading of your author, and that your own writings, whether you like it or not, show that you have the same sense of shame: for your naturally good disposition would not permit you to utter obscenity therein. [148][7]

Now, it is true that Christine first speaks of the blushing queens in the letter to Montreuil, but she reiterates the point in her letter to Pierre Col, and it is only in this latter letter, of course, that she twits him about his own writings:

---

and of Christine's letter to the Queen, for the correct dating of London MS. Harl. 4431 and MS. Bibl. nat. fr. 12779 as *mil cccc et ung*.

[4] *Der Streit um den Rosenroman* (Munich: Wilhelm Fink Verlag, 1972). See especially pp. 47-179.

[5] For example, Piaget, Dow, Ward, Potansky.

[6] For the complete text of Gerson's letter, see pages 145-152.

[7] This and all succeeding numbers bracketed in the text of this introduction refer to page numbers in this volume.

But you who assert by so many arguments that Master
Jean de Meun's Reason is right in saying that they [the
secret members] should be called openly by name, I ask
you sincerely ... why you do not name them openly in
your own writing without beating around the bush? [123]

Surely, Gerson's remark stems from, and is therefore later than,
this one. With this change then, the chronological scheme is as
follows:

I.	May 1399	Christine de Pisan, *L'Epistre au Dieu d'Amours*
II.	Late 1400 or beginning 1401	Jean de Montreuil, *Treatise* (now lost)
III.	Early 1401	Jean de Montreuil, Letter, *Cum ut dant sese res*
IV.	1401, mid-year	Jean de Montreuil, Letter, *Quo magis*
V.	1401, mid-year	Jean de Montreuil, Letter, *Etsi facundissimus*
VI.	1401, before Sept. 13, 1401	Christine de Pisan, Letter to Jean de Montreuil
VII.	Sept. 13, 1401	Gontier Col, Letter to Christine de Pisan
VIII.	Sept. 15, 1401	Gontier Col, Letter to Christine de Pisan
IX.	October 1401	Christine de Pisan, Letter to Gontier Col
X.	Feb. 1, 1402	Christine de Pisan, Letter to the Queen
XI.	Feb. 1, 1402	Christine de Pisan, Letter to Guillaume de Tignonville
XII.	May 18, 1402	Jean Gerson, *Traité against the Roman de la Rose*
XIII.	Between the beginning of June and beginning of Sept. 1402	Pierre Col, Letter to Christine de Pisan
XIV.	Oct. 2, 1402	Christine de Pisan, Letter to Pierre Col
XV.	Oct. (?), 1402	Jean Gerson, Letter to Pierre Col

XVI.   Between the begin- Jean de Montreuil, Letter, *Ut sunt*
       ning of October   *mores*
       and the begin-
       ning of Decem-
       ber, 1402

XVII. Before the begin- Jean de Montreuil, Letter, *Ex quo*
       ning of Decem-   *nuge*
       ber, 1402

XVIII. Dec. 17, 1402   Jean Gerson, Sermon, *Poenitemini:*
                          Par le merveilleux

XIX.   Between Dec. 17   Pierre Col, Letter to Christine de
       and 24, 1402   Pisan

XX.   Dec. 24, 1402   Jean Gerson, Sermon, *Poenitemini:*
                          En benoiste journee

XXI.   End of Dec., 1402 Jean de Montreuil, Letter, *Scis me*

XXII. Dec. 31, 1402   Jean Gerson, Sermon, *Poenitemini:*
                          Bien a point et appropos

Five documents included here are not strictly a part of the correspondence proper. The first, *L'Epistre au Dieu d'Amours,* contains the earliest remarks on the *Roman de la Rose* by one of the contenders in the Quarrel and is, in fact, specifically mentioned by Christine in her first letter. Relevant portions only have been translated. The second is Document XII, Jean Gerson's *Traité,* a sort of literary, allegorical *disputatio,* which, despite its conventional suspension of decision, is heavily weighted against the *Rose.* This document, though not itself in the form of a letter, is nevertheless an integral part of the correspondence, receiving as it does an elaborate and detailed reply from Pierre Col. Finally, the three sermons by Gerson (Documents XVIII, XX, XXII), or rather relevant portions of them, are included to indicate something of the widespread interest in and knowledge of the Quarrel.

As can be seen from the above listing, Christine de Pisan, a "mere woman," as earlier critics sometimes liked to style her,[8] played a leading role in the debate. Those earlier critics, however,

---

[8] See, e.g., Lula McDowell Richardson's curiously titled *The Forerunners of Feminism in French Literature of the Renaissance from Christine of Pisa to Marie de Gournay,* Diss. Johns Hopkins (Baltimore: Johns Hopkins University Press, 1929), p. 15.

tended to overexaggerate and misinterpret the significance of Christine's contribution to the debate. Christine was seen as a woman
far ahead of her time, the first defender of *les droits féminins,* the
herald of equality between the sexes; and her role in the Querelle
was judged accordingly. [9] Inevitably, reaction to such views set in,
and, as usual, reaction tends to become overreaction and distorts
even as it seeks to correct distortion. Thus a recent and highly-
regarded scholarly work on the *Roman de la Rose* informs us flatly
that one should not take Christine de Pisan's contribution "too
seriously." Her role in the debate, we are informed, "has been
rather inflated, one suspects, by modern feminists . . ." [10] Earlier,
D. W. Robertson, Jr., who through his notable *Preface to Chaucer*
has exerted a powerful influence on modern views of the Quarrel,
dismissed Christine slightingly as an "irate woman" with "frenzied
observations." [11] Further, Rosamond Tuve viewed Christine's part
in the debate, according to John Fleming, as only a kind of elaborate
joke, a half-comic pose adopted for the moment without serious
intent. [12] Such observations seem to represent the modern scholarly
view — though perhaps one should add Princetonian to the qualify-
ing adjectives — of the *Querelle de la Rose.*

Now, it may indeed be true that earlier critics tended to "inflate"
Christine's role in the Quarrel, but the later ones can scarcely be
said to have been more moderate. For if the earlier critics distorted
the facts somewhat in Christine's favor, the later ones have been
all too cavalier in dismissing her usually sound, and almost always

---

[9] See W. Minto, "A Champion of her Sex," *MacMillan's Magazine,* 53
(1886), 264-275; L. Abensour, *La Femme et le féminisme avant la Révolution*
(Paris: E. Leroux, 1923), pp. v-vi.

[10] John V. Fleming, *The Roman de la Rose: A Study in Allegory and
Iconography* (Princeton: Princeton University Press, 1969), p. 47. The following remarks about the quality of the arguments of the contenders in the
debate have been published in a slightly differing form in *The French Review,*
48 (1974), 298-307.

[11] (Princeton: Princeton University Press, 1962), p. 364.

[12] See Fleming, *Roman,* p. 47. Fleming fails to document his source for
for this statement. In "Hoccleve's 'Letter of Cupid' and the 'Quarrel' over the
Roman de la Rose," Medium Aevum, 40 (1971), 29, Fleming repeats even
more forcefully his understanding that Rosamond Tuve thought of Christine's
posture in the Quarrel as "largely whimsical" — again without documentation.
Rosamond Tuve, of course, speaks of the Quarrel in *Allegorical Imagery: Some
Mediaeval Books and their Posterity* (Princeton: Princeton University Press,
1966). See especially p. 274 and note 19.

quite charming, arguments out of hand. There is simply no evidence to suggest that Christine treated the whole affair as a sort of whimsical jest. For although she can be airily and wittily humorous in defense of her views, as in her delightful adaptation of the humility formula at the end of her first letter [56], she is at the same time deadly serious. And if, for example, Gerson, whose seriousness no one questions, can protest that he would not pray for the soul of his own brother if he were to die an unrepentant disciple of Meun [152], Christine can, with equal gravity, use the example of her own son to score a point in the debate [127]. Furthermore, of all the extant documents of the debate, Christine's contribution far exceeds that of any other writer; Christine, in fact, wrote just slightly less than all the other writers combined, including her ally Gerson. This seems to be a curiously extended bit of insouciance. One would do better, perhaps, to argue the light indifference of, say, Gontier Col, who apparently relinquished his pen to his brother, Pierre, after only two brief letters. Moreover, in her reply to Pierre Col, Christine argues *in extenso,* answering him point by point, in an expansive and minutely detailed letter. Such careful attention to her opponent's argument scarcely suggests levity on her part. It is true that in this letter Christine whimsically compares the arguments of the defenders and opponents to the vain efforts of alchemists [125], but this simile reveals more her feeling, at this late point in the debate, of the uselessness in reasoning with the prejudices of her opponents than her own lack of seriousness in the discussion. Further, outside the debate correspondence proper, Christine returns repeatedly to the question of the *Rose*: she refers slightingly to Meun in *Le Débat de Deux Amans*; she writes *L'Espistre au Dieu d'Amours,* which, later, in sixteenth-century France was to be generally known by the title of *Le Contre Romant de la Rose*; and she sets up a new order of the Rose in honor of ladies in *Le Dit de la Rose*. Finally, any opinion of her half-heartedness in the affair should be completely dispelled by Christine's inspired decision to send, along with an accompanying, explanatory letter, a collection of the *Rose* correspondence to the Queen.

It will not do, on the other hand, to see Christine as a kind of vociferous fourteenth-century women's liberationist. As a recent critic has commented, "She was unable, so far as I know, to question the established inferiority of women to men. But she could admonish men to do what they were supposed to do, and were largely failing to do to a distressing degree about 1400 . . ." [13] Christine looks backward rather than forward; she is conservative (one might almost say reactionary), not revolutionary. She looks back with nostalgia to the medieval *cours d'amours* and to idealized chivalry, and if such never did ever really exist, that fact does not, of course, lessen the force of her vision.

With regard to the outcome of the debate, history was obviously on the side of the defenders of Meun, and it is this fact apparently which occasions the abrupt dismissal of the arguments of the opponents, though a proper disinterest would suggest that such an historical circumstance is irrelevant to the quality of the arguments on either side. Nevertheless, the standard critical opinion seems to be that the formidable defenders of Meun absolutely win the day. John Fleming, for example, has not only discounted Christine's seriousness but has also harshly criticized the quality of her arguments by repeating Jean de Montreuil's slander at face value: "Taken seriously, her arguments and her manner show the acumen (in the words of Jean de Montreuil) of 'the Greek whore who dared to write against Theophrastus.' " [14] Nor does Fleming display any more respect for Jean Gerson's contribution to the debate: "To any disinterested student, it is apparent that Gerson was thoroughly trounced in the Quarrel . . ." [15] A similar opinion about Christine's forensic abilities was expressed recently by Raymond Kilgour, who remarks that Gerson came to Christine's aid "when she was being overwhelmed by the defenders of the *Roman de la Rose.*" [16] Thus in the *Querelle de la Rose,* it appears, Gerson was

---

[13] F. Douglas Kelly, "Reflections on the Role of Christine de Pisan as a Feminist Writer," *Sub-Stance,* 2 (1972), 63-71. See also Richardson, *The Forerunners,* p. 33, who writes that there is nothing in Christine's writings which "could give anyone grounds for calling Christine a radical feminist. Rather, she is a woman resentful of the injustice done her sex, and desirous of reestablishing its virtues and worth in the eyes of her contemporaries. She does not demand for woman as complete an education as for man, nor does she feel that it is legitimate for a woman to aspire to all of man's occupations."

[14] *The Roman,* p. 47. The quotation from Montreuil may be seen in document XVI of this volume.

[15] *The Roman,* p. 47.

[16] *The Decline of Chivalry as Shown in the French Literature of the Late Middle Ages* (Gloucester, Mass.: Peter Smith, 1966), p. 180.

"trounced," while Christine, before Gerson's intervention, was "being overwhelmed." A strong case could, in fact, be made for quite the opposite. Montreuil's harsh invective about the "Greek whore" is a case in point. It is the supporters of Meun who become stridently defensive, who display a distinct sense of uneasiness, who, in their obstinate refusal to admit the slightest fault in their *auctor,* overstate and overstress (and therefore weaken) their case, and who, consequently, have resort to *argumentum ad hominem.* Christine speaks of her opponents with respect and defers to their rhetorical ability, and although there is frequently a large element of the ironic in her tone, she never becomes harshly personal. She does, it is true, argue *ad hominem* against Jean de Meun — "But truly since he blamed all women in general, I am constrained to believe that he never had acquaintance of, or regular contact with, any honorable or virtuous woman" [52] — but with her immediate opponents she addresses herself to the facts of their arguments, not to personal matters. In contrast, Pierre Col lapses into anti-feminism — "Oh excessively foolish pride! Oh opinion uttered too quickly and thoughtlessly by the mouth of a woman! A woman who condemns a man of high understanding," etc. [103] — and accuses Christine of glory-seeking motives — "O God glorious! How many people there are who have never craved fame for themselves, or who blame themselves somewhat in order to glorify themselves! This is why you call yourself a small branch" [161]. Gontier Col speaks of her in the same manner as a woman impassioned, presumptuous, and arrogant [60], for which Christine reproaches him: "you wrote in a fit of impatience your second, more offensive letter, reproaching my feminine sex, which you describe as impassioned by nature" [62] and asks him to "please do not willfully choose to reproach and reprove my true opinion, honestly arrived at, just because it is not to your pleasure" [62]. Moreover, Montreuil is clearly ill at ease in his feeling that he has been "badly treated and censured most bitterly by school men of no little authority, more than you would believe" [165]. All of this surely has little of the triumphant ring that one would like to hear from those who have been clearly victorious in the debate.

Two basic assumptions, apparently, underlie the recent harsh criticism of the opposers of Meun: that they are squeamishly puritanical in their approach to matters sexual, with the accompanying, though unacknowledged, corollary that such an attitude, *ipso facto,* produces poor argument; and that they are unwilling or unable to recognize the dramatic quality of the *Roman de la Rose.* The first, stated thus baldly with all its implications acknowledged, can be dismissed immediately as a clear non-sequitur. The arguments against the *Roman de la Rose* are indeed from a moral standpoint; they are at the same time, as will be demonstrated, quite effective. The second is more substantial and reasonable, but the charge is unfair in direct proportion to the neglect of the first principle, the moral viewpoint of the writers. It is not true that Christine and Gerson do not recognize the dramatic quality of the *Roman de la Rose,* that is, make distinctions between the author speaking in *propria persona* and dramatic speeches by his invented characters. They recognize this principle very well, and it would be greatly surprising if they did not, since Christine herself wrote such dramatic poems and Gerson was well known for speaking through "characters" in his sermons. [17] They are simply unwilling to allow that such a principle gives absolute licence to a writer. The defense that Meun merely put into the mouths of his *dramatis personae* words appropriate to their character is, Gerson writes, far too slight for so great a crime [80]. For, as he goes on to explain, such a position opens the way to every kind of lubricious, heretical, or treasonous writing, and it is especially reprehensible in Meun because, as he remarks, "Everything seems to be said in his own person; everything seems as true as the Gospel, particularly to those foolish and vicious lovers to whom he speaks" [81]. And granted the premises — however distasteful to our modern age — such a moral argument is beyond reproach. Moreover, Gerson asserts that heedless of his own dramatic framework, Meun in many places projects his own views onto his characters [89]. Christine makes a similar argument: "You respond to Lady Eloquence and me that Master Jean de Meun introduced characters in his book, and made each one speak fittingly, according to what pertained to him. I readily admit that the proper equipment is necessary for any particular game, but the will of the player manipulates such equipment to his own purpose. And it is clearly true (may it not dis-

---

[17] See James L. Connolly, *John Gerson, Reformer and Mystic* (Louvain: Uystpruyst, 1928), p. 119, and cf. Document XX of this volume.

please you) that he was at fault in attributing to some of his characters functions which do not properly belong to them" [130]. That Christine and Gerson do not make careful distinctions between the author and his characters throughout their arguments is, from their point of view, irrelevant. Immoral speeches — without clear, unambiguous disapproval in the context — are to be condemned, whoever says them. "I would wish," Gerson writes, "that this Foolish Lover had not used these characters, except as Holy Scripture did, that is, to reprove evil, in such a way that every man might perceive that condemnation of evil and that approbation of good, and (what is most important) that all those things could have been done without excessive frivolity" [81]. And in another context he writes, "we censure not characters but writings" [150].

Pierre Col's argument, on the other hand, is just as much based on moral grounds as that of his opponents — it is simply, one feels, less sincere, filled with special pleading. Col has been put, as it were, on the moral defensive and therefore feels impelled to expound Meun's moral purpose, but he is just not Robertsonian enough, despite what one might feel from a reading of Fleming, to be absolutely convincing. Jean de Meun wrote the whole long process, he informs us, in order to teach women how to guard the "castle" better: "If Jean de Meun has described the way in which it [the castle] was captured, has he not given a great advantage to the castle guards by showing them how it was captured, so that they may in the future block the gap or place better guards there and thus lessen the chances of the assailants" [108]. Ovid wrote his book in Latin, "which women did not understand" [108], and therefore taught only the assailants, but Meun wrote in the vernacular and thus "the more varied the forms of attack that he describes the better he teaches the defenders to guard the castle: and it was for this purpose that he wrote it" [109]. Does the book contain scurrilous words which seem to degrade women? It does so merely because he quoted other authors, and he makes use of them only "in order to teach more effectively how gatekeepers should guard the castle" [109]. Such strained reasoning, of course, reveals less Col's conviction than his uneasiness with Meun's scurrility, and his opponents very well know it. To Col's defense of the use of the word "sanctuaries" for the sexual organs, for example, Christine retorts sharply, "certainly, you are not saying what you think, begging your pardon" [120].

But surely it is a more important matter for modern critics — and more pertinent to this particular work — to be concerned with the quality of the arguments on both sides, rather than to attempt a decision about the winner of the debate. Even disregarding the historical and literary importance of the quarrel, the exchange is delightful and interesting in its own right. An example of the changes on the ancient topos of the humility formula by both Pierre Col and Christine, for example, will suggest something of their lightness of touch and amused self-awareness, as well as their skill, even in the midst of their conventional protests of inadequacy. At the end of her first letter, Christine writes:

> And may it not be imputed to me as folly, arrogance, or presumption, that I, a woman, should dare to reproach and call into question so subtle an author, and to diminish the stature of his work, when he alone, a man, has dared to undertake to defame and blame without exception an entire sex. [56]

But Pierre Col can manage a similar feat, and one wonders whether he is not mocking Christine's rhetorical device with his own:

> May my coming forth to defend him not be considered presumptuous or arrogant, for in truth I would never be guilty of such. Rather, I simply desire to be, at least, the least among the disciples of the aforesaid Meun. And since your argument against him is so weak that there is no need of a greater, I do not speak for the most advanced disciples of the aforesaid Meun, but rather for the middle or for those near the bottom, where your argument belongs. [93]

Aside from his occasional strained moral pleading then, Pierre Col does indeed, as his modern advocates claim for him, write a witty, forceful argument. Fleming has given the title of the first "modern" critic of the *Roman de la Rose* to Gerson,[18] but, in a different sense from that intended by Fleming, that honor best

---

[18] *The Roman,* p. 47. "Modern," i.e., the development of a non-medieval sense of shame toward the "secret members," etc. The idea, however, was originally voiced by Robertson, *Preface,* p. 361.

belongs to Pierre Col. Unlike his opponents, who do not do so at all, he quotes extensively from the *Roman de la Rose* to substantiate the points he makes, and modern criticism has borne out his belief that the *Roman de la Rose* was not intended by the vain "dits" which Jean de Meun repents of in his *Testament*. [19] Like a true literary critic, he emphasizes over and again that the *Roman de la Rose* is a fully dramatic work and that a character's opinion must not be confused with the author's; *Le Jaloux* speaks as a *jaloux,* not as Meun. Once and once only, he argues, does Jean de Meun speak as Jean de Meun in the poem, and he quotes him in defense of the work [113] — and misses, perhaps chooses to miss, the delicious irony of Meun's "defense."

The most charming quality of Pierre Col's argument is the obvious delight he took in writing it. You say, he writes Christine, that it was all right to name the secret members in the State of Innocence. Now, I ask you, would you call by name the secret members of a two- or three-year old child, for "*he* is in the state of innocence" [94]? Or those of an aged man "who has been chaste and virginal all his life" [94]? Or those of the dumb beasts, "for they do not sin at all" [94]? Moreover, "if the pollution of our first parents made the secret members so shameful that one is not permitted to name them, I say that by a stronger reason one ought not to call our first parents by name. For they are the ones who sinned; not their members" [94]. It is such verbal ingenuity, I fear, which has seduced the modern critics. Nevertheless, Col is more witty than wise, more diverting than convincing, in his lively riposte — to the great detriment, of course, to his argument, however delightful in itself. In his remarks about the State of Innocence he has, of course, changed terms in mid-argument by lightly shifting from capital to lower-case letters — i.e., from State of Innocence to state of innocence — and has therefore, as Gerson points out, caught himself in the Pelagian heresy, "like birds caught in lime, entangling themselves more and more by their efforts to escape" [146]. And with regard to the sin of "our first parents," Christine innocently poses him this "serious problem, which I would be glad to have you solve for me. Why was it that as soon as our first parents had sinned and had knowledge of good and evil, they hid

---

[19] See Fleming, *The Roman,* p. 49.

their secret members immediately and became ashamed, although they had not yet made use of them? I ask you why they did not cover their eyes or their mouths, with which they had sinned, rather than their secret members? It seems to me that at that moment reasonable shame was born, which you and your accomplices, as well as the character your master named Reason, wish to hunt down and destroy" [118]. "A simple little housewife sustained by the doctrine of Holy Church," she later remarks, "could criticize your error" [130].

This, clearly, is no one-sided debate. The opponents of Meun argue cogently, forcibly, as well as wittily in defense of their position. Note how effectively, for example, Christine picks up one of Pierre Col's *faux pas* and turns it into a weapon: in her first letter, Christine had argued strongly against the *Roman de la Rose* line "In the amorous war, it is better to deceive than to be deceived," and Col defended it vigorously in his answer. He then undercut his own defense, however, by weakly ending with the reflection that he had always thought that it may well have been interpolated into the text [103], leaving himself wide open for Christine's attack. "But lest I forget," she writes, "I will say now what does please me in your remarks: that is, that you believe Master Jean de Meun never wrote this in his book at all, but that it was interpolated. It seems clear that you say this because you wish it to be so (saving your grace), for this passage is in the same language and the same style, but you wish very much that he had never said it. You can right boldly say that such words were never utterd by Reason, the daughter of God! " [126].

Moreover, Christine is clever enough to take Col's main point of attack — that Meun speaks through characters and not in his own person — and turn it on him: "And thus I believe that Master Jean de Meun most certainly did not say these words through her [the Old Woman] in order to praise marriage, for this was never her function. And I remind you that you previously asserted that this was not Meun speaking, but his characters, each in his own role. But here it was he who said this good word! and there it was not he who spoke in the chapter of the Jealous Man! First you say one thing and then another" [139]. Or note the way in which she turns Pierre Col's own self-adopted title of the especial disciple of Meun into a weapon against him:

But you who assert by so many arguments that Master Jean de Meun's Reason is right in saying that they should be called openly by name, I ask you sincerely, you who are his very especial disciple as you say, why you do not name them openly in your own writing without beating around the bush? It seems to me that you are not a good pupil, for you do not follow well at all the doctrine of your master, who teaches you to name them. If you say that this is not customary, are you then afraid of being criticized, so that you take heed to this custom? Do you wish to live by the opinion of other people? Rather, follow good doctrine, in order to show them what they ought to do, for all things must begin somewhere. And if someone blames you at first, you will be praised for it later, when people see that the custom is good and right. [109-110]

But perhaps Christine's delicate play on words in her remarks about the alchemists will best illustrate her ability to turn a phrase: "You quote; I reply. And when we have worked and worked, it is all worth nothing. For the matter [*la matière*] is very dishonorable, much like certain alchemists who think they can transmute dung" [125]. Surely, Christine is punning on the word *la matière* — the "matter," that is, the "subject" in hand, and the "matière," that is, the "materiel" of the alchemists, which, we discover at the end of the sentence, is *fiens,* "dung." Thus in the very midst of her protestations of inability to persuade, the woman who disavows facility with words or *bel rhetorique* can so manage it that the scatological *matière* influences and contaminates the "matter," that is, the *Roman de la Rose.* Then she can quietly add, "I would prefer not to be an alchemist in this affair" [125]. Would that all moralists were equally as witty.

Nor is Gerson as inept as we have been led to believe. Pierre Col, for example, had written that the Bible teaches us that it was customary to sanctify the secret members of a woman [97]. To this, Gerson replied acidly, "But when you add that the secret members of women were formerly sanctified by custom, I do not know what kind of Bible taught you, unless perhaps you had one in your possession different from ours" [147]. In the same vein he can twit Col with the fact that Christine, that manly woman — *virago* is Gerson's word — had pressed him so hard that he had felt compelled to suggest an interpolation into the *Roman de la Rose.* And to Col's serious use of Meun's comic, sophistical apology to women that he himself does not cricize women, that he merely quotes others who did, Gerson sensibly replies:

> Wherefore, you his admirers, do not seek to praise him if he spoke well, since he himself, in bringing controversial matters into the book, denies responsibility for wicked words which might bring shame on it. Do not, therefore, grow so hot with passion in hatred against us, and do not declaim against us with such bombastic words and swelled-out cheeks, if this book is guilty in its own right. For we censure not characters but writings (whoever made them), since one who gives a poisoned drink, even if it is mixed by someone else, must not be judged free of guilt on that account. [150]

Finally, Christine has the good sense not to overstate her case, but even her concessions are turned to good account. "My judgment concedes that Master Jean de Meun was a very great, learned, and eloquent clerk," but the more's the pity, for he "would have been able to produce so much better a work, more profitable, and of higher sentiment, if he had applied himself to it, and that he did not do so is great loss" [54]. And "I do not condemn the *Roman de la Rose* entirely, for it does indeed contain some good things, and its style is poetically pleasing, but therein lies the greater peril, for the more authentic the good the more faith one puts in the evil" [54]. Beside such adroit maneuverings, certainly, the extravagances of the Cols — "Master Jean de Meun, true Catholic, worthy master . . . most profound and excellent philosopher, knowing all that to human understanding is knowable" [57] [20] — sound hollow indeed.

Enough has been said perhaps to indicate the tenor of the *débat.* Despite the impression left by critics, particularly with regard to the opponents of Meun, the *Querelle de la Rose* is not a collection of dry, insipid, and poorly argued documents, interesting only from an historical standpoint. Completely aside from what they tell us about the fifteenth-century view of one of the most important works of the Middle Ages, and aside from their worth as indicators of a shift in cultural, literary, or moral taste — as

---

[20] The words are Gontier Col's. Similar sentiments could, however, be quoted from Pierre Col. For example, see page 92 of this volume.

D. W. Robertson argues — the letters are a delight to read in and of themselves, fascinating in their own right. Yet such qualities are difficult to appreciate. Old French is quite deceptive in appearance; because of semantic ambiguities, it is a difficult language, even to the putative experts, a fact which accounts in part perhaps for the many misconceptions about the debate. Nor have the scholars always acquitted themselves well with the Latin documents. The primary aims of the present translation thus have always been clarity and precision, as accurate a rendering of the sense as possible, even when this involved what we lightly called during the course of our work "shuffling and re-dealing," a total dissolution and re-organization of a lengthy, extremely complex sentence or group of sentences. At the same time we have attempted to preserve, as far as possible, the flavor of the original, but this effort has almost always been in terms of form and structure rather than vocabulary. We have sought to avoid archaisms and Renaissance English, despite their appeal to translators of fifteenth-century documents. We have, however, preserved certain "quaint" expressions, for which there is no exact equivalent in Modern English. "Saving your grace," for example, sometimes appears in the text, because "begging your pardon" (although we sometimes employed it as an alternate) can scarcely render the delicate shades of simultaneous deference and opposition. An example will perhaps best illustrate what is meant by preservation of original tone in terms of structure rather than vocabulary. Gontier Col begins his first letter to Christine in the following way:

> Femme de hault et esleué entendement, digne d'onneur et recommendacions grans, j'ay ouy parler par la bouche de pluseurs notables clers que entre tes aultres estudes et euures vertueuses moult a louer, comme ie entens par leur relacion, tu as nouuellement escript par maniere de inuective aucunement contre ce que mon maistre, enseigneur et familier feu maistre Jehan de Meun, vray catholique, solennel maistre, et docteur en son temps en saincte theologie, philosophe tresperfont et excellent, sachant tout ce qui a entendement humain est scible, duquel la gloire et renommee vit et viura es aages a venir entre les entendemens par ses merites leuez par grace de dieu et euure de nature, fist et compila ou liure de la Rose.[21]

---

[21] Ward, *The Epistles,* p. 29.

We have rendered this in one long sentence as follows:

> Woman of high and exalted understanding, worthy of
> honor and great esteem, I have heard say from many no-
> table clerks that among your other studies and virtuous
> and praiseworthy works, as I understand by their remarks,
> you have recently written a kind of invective against the
> book of the *Rose* composed by my master, teacher, and
> friend, the lamented Master Jean de Meun, true Catholic,
> worthy master, and, in his time, doctor of holy theology,
> a most profound and excellent philosopher, knowing all
> that to human understanding is knowable, whose glory and
> fame lives and will live in the ages to come among under-
> standing men, elevated by his merits, by the grace of God,
> and by the work of Nature. [57]

To have interrupted the flow of this long opening period, by im-
posing modern grammatical structure on it, would have been detri-
mental, we felt, not only to tone but also to sense, because something of Col's feeling for Meun is, surely, imparted by the mere
piling up of ideas and epithets in this free-flowing sentence.

A note about the texts. There is yet today no scholarly edition
of all the letters and documents in the Quarrel. The nearest thing
to a complete text is Charles F. Ward's 1911 much-flawed edition,
which, to mention its most egregrious error, prints the Latin text
of Jean Gerson's *Tractatus contra Romantium de Rosa* as if it were
from the hand of Gerson himself. Modern scholarship has shown
—and this fact was well known before the time of Ward's edition—
that this text is a late Latin translation by someone unknown (certainly not Gerson) of a *Traité* or *Vision* written by Gerson in
French. Pierre Col quotes verbatim from the French *Traité,* and
Gerson remarks that he by no means intends to translate it into
Latin [145].[22] Ward, moreover, does not give the text of the
famous letter in which Montreuil compares Christine to the "Greek
whore," and with regard to the other Latin letters of Montreuil
that Ward publishes, "it seems fitting to me," Ornato writes, "to

---

[22] For further evidence that the Latin *Tractatus* is not from Gerson's hand,
see Langlois, "Le Traité de Gerson contre Le Roman de la Rose," *Romania,*
45 (1919), 23-48. Yet see Françoise du Castel, *Damoiselle Christine de Pizan:
Veuve de Mᵉ Etienne de Castel,* 1364-1431 (Paris: Editions A. et J. Picard,
1972), p. 53, who continues to propagate the old error.

underline that the word 'pubblicare' is understood here in its narrowest sense, and means 'to reproduce exactly a preceding edition.' Naturally, as always happens, the reproduction turns out still worse than the original, which in our case, presents indeed, in its turn, more than a few errors." [23] In short, these Latin texts are highly unreliable. The Old French letters, edited by Ward from the MSS., are, while not totally free from error, much more trustworthy.

The present translation, therefore, makes use of Ward as a basic text for the French documents, with the exception of Gerson's sermons and, of course, his *Traité*. The translators, however, have turned to MSS. Bibliothèque nationale française 835 and 1563 for clarification of specific passages. [24] Also, owing to the generosity and graciousness of Professor Erik Hicks, we have had the very good fortune of being able to consult in MS. Hicks' forthcoming edition of the French letters. For *Le Traité de Gerson contre Le Roman de la Rose,* we have relied on the text by Ernest Langlois, published in *Romania,* 45 (1919), 23-48. The translations of Montreuil's letters are from the texts in Ezio Ornato's edition, *Jean de Montreuil, Opera* (Torino: G. Giappichelli, 1963), vol. I, Letters 103, 118, 120, 122, 152, 154. And the excerpts from Christine de Pisan's *Epistre au Dieu d'Amours* are from *Œuvres Poétiques de Christine de Pisan,* ed. Maurice Roy, SATF 24 (1886; rpt. New York: Johnson Reprint Corporation, 1965), II, 10-14. The translations of Gerson's sermons are based on the texts in *Jean Gerson, Œuvres complètes,* ed. Mgr. Glorieux (Paris: Desclée & Cie, 1968), vol. VII, Nos. 370, 371, 373. The bracketed numbers to the side of our translated texts refer to the page numbers of these editions.

---

[23] Jean de Montreuil, *Opera,* ed. Ezio Ornato (Torino: G. Giappichelli, 1963), I, page lxvii. "... mi sembra opportuno sottolineare che il vocabolo 'pubblicare' va inteso qui nella sua accezione più angusta, e significa 'riprodurre esattamente un' edizione precedente.' Naturalmente, come sempre accade, la riproduzione risulta ancora peggiore dell' originale, il quale, nel nostro caso, presenta già, a sua volta, non poche scorrettezze."

[24] On pages 85 and 86 of Ward's text of Christine's reply to Pierre Col and on page 70 of Pierre Col's first letter to Christine, for example, appear three different sets of unnoted and unexplained marks of elision. These correspond to nothing in the MSS. — no lacuna of any kind. The reading of the MSS. continues without a break. Ward has apparently used the elision marks as an indication of what he felt was a gap in the sense. Ward is highly unreliable also in his explanatory footnotes. For Col's remark about the Bible prohibiting castrated men from entering a church, for example, he cites Leviticus XXI, instead of the correct Deuteronomy XXIII.1.

Finally, there is no need, perhaps, in this age of quick Ph.D.'s and de-emphasis on the value of languages even among medievalists, to justify a translation of these documents. But we might note our general feeling, nevertheless, that a literary debate of this kind will hold the interest of a wider range of scholars than just narrow specialists, and indeed deserves a larger audience than has generally been the case because of language barriers. Moreover, there have been a number of erroneous and misleading statements made about the debate, even by the putative specialists, [25] and the present work will, we hope, correct such false impressions. [26]

Debts of gratitude have accumulated during the process of this work, and we would like to extend our sincere thanks to the following people especially: to Giuseppe Baglivi, Instructor of Italian at Kent State University, for advice and suggestions with regard to Italian and Latin; to Garrett McCutchan, Instructor of Italian and French at Kent State University, for the same and for many delightful hours of poring over certain difficult Latin passages; to

---

[25] The classic error, of course, is A. Coville's, who read three "contradicteurs" into the phrase *nudius tertius* ("day before yesterday") and then went on to argue that these three were Jean Gerson, Christine de Pisan, and Guillaume de Tignonville. Even the noted scholar Johan Huizinga tends to lead the unwary reader astray. He reports Montreuil as asserting that "several of the most learned and enlightened men honor the *Roman de la Rose* so much that their appreciation resembles a cult (*paene ut colerent*), and that they would rather do without their shirt than his book," when the most that can be derived from Montreuil's crabbed and opaque Latin is "*it is pointless to pretend* that you and many other worthy and learned men have shown the book to be of such worth that they ought to honor it so much that they would rather do without their shirt than this book." Further examples of Huizinga's lack of precision might be advanced. In his efforts to prove the "blasphemy" and "impious mysticism" of Pierre Col, Huizinga is generally misleading. It is somewhat less than accurate, for example, to state unequivocally that "Pierre Col had not scrupled to affirm that the Song of Solomon was composed in honour of the daughter of Pharaoh," when Col merely notes that "some teachers [*aucuns docteurs*] even say that Solomon made the Canticles on account of his love of Pharaoh's daughter." [100]. Similarly, Huizinga's remark that Col had "predicted that Gerson himself would fall madly in love" is rather distant from Col's more modest question, "And is it not possible that even he in the future may be a foolish lover?" [101]. See *The Waning of the Middle Ages* (London: Edward Arnold & Co., 1937), pp. 104-106.

[26] This book has been delayed in press for some four years, and has therefore inevitably dated. Eric Hicks' fine edition of the documents, for example, *Le Debat sur le Roman de la Rose* (Paris: Champion, 1977), has since appeared.

James Cooney, Assistant Professor of English at Kent State University, for reading and commenting on our translations from Latin; to Jan Nelson, Professor, University of Alabama, for his careful reading and commentary on Christine's first letter and Gerson's *Traité*; to Esther Grant, Associate Professor of German at Kent State University, for her enthusiastic interest in our work and advice with regard to Montreuil's letters; to Professor Avalle-Arce, University of North Carolina, for his thoughtful and meticulous reading of our MS. and his invaluable assistance and commentary; and most especially to Erik C. Hicks for his very thorough and careful reading and criticism of our work. Appreciation is due also to Professor Martin Nurmi, Chairman of the English Department at Kent State University, for a reduction of teaching load to further this work. The Universiy Research Office of Kent State University has furnished funds unstintingly in payment for microfilm, xeroxing, typing, etc., for which we are grateful. Mrs. Lee Stockdale, Administrative Assistant of the Kent State University English Office, has been extremely kind and helpful in numerous ways, as has also Mrs. Margaret Boosinger, secretary. We are grateful too to Anna Gasbarro and Diane Salloy, Graduate Assistants in the English Department of Kent State University, who saved the translators long hours of tedious work by their generous efforts. And, finally we owe much to the Kent State University Library Interlibrary Loan Service, ably managed by Mrs. Jane Benson, and especially to her two assistants, Cathy Ake and Bill Miller.

We are indebted to the following publishers for permission to use printed materials: to *The French Review* for use, in a somewhat differing form, of the article entitled "*La Querelle de la Rose*: In Defense of the Opponents," printed in volume 48 (1974), 298-307; and to Desclée & Cie for permission to quote from *Jean Gerson, Œuvres complètes* (1968), vol. 7.

LETTERS AND DOCUMENTS

I

CHRISTINE DE PISAN
EPISTRE AU DIEU D'AMOURS [EXCERPTS]

*[Although not a part of the debate proper, this poem, which was
written in 1399, contains the earliest adverse criticism of Jean
de Meun by Christine de Pisan, and is for that reason worthy
of inclusion here. This could, in fact, have been the stimulus to
the informal discussions on the* Rose *that Christine mentions
later, and therefore ultimately of the debate itself. The text of
the poem may be consulted in* Œuvres Poetiques de Christine
de Pisan, *ed. Maurice Roy, SATF 24 (1886; rpt. New York:
Johnson Reprint Corporation, 1965), II, 10-14.]*

In his book *The Remedy of Love,* Ovid said many evil things about
women — and, I think, wrongly. He accused them of immorality,
leading lives full of filth, ugliness, and wickedness. I deny that they
have such vices, and I promise to champion them against anyone
who may throw down the gauntlet: I mean, of course, honorable
women — I include no worthless ones in my account.

... ...

[281-290]

If someone says that we ought to believe books written by reputable men of sound judgment, men who never deigned to lie but
who nevertheless demonstrated the wickedness of women, my reaction is that such authors have never sought to do anything but
deceive women. They cannot get enough of them; every day they
seek fresh ones, and yet they are unfaithful even to the most
beautiful. How many did David have, or King Solomon? And God
was angry with them and punished them for their misconduct.

Many other men, like Ovid, who held such a grudge against women, set out to slander them. And all the other clerks who spoke so much against them were, more than other men, maddened by lust, not for a single woman only but for thousands of them. Now, if such men had ladies or wives who did not obey their bidding or who strove to deceive them, what is so strange about that? For there can be no doubt that when a man plunges into such vileness, he certainly does not seek out well-bred ladies or reputable women: he neither knows them nor has anything to do with them. He wants only those who suit his purpose, prostitutes and whores. Is a debauché worthy to possess anything of value? Such a man pursues all women and then believes he has thoroughly concealed his shame by condemning them with his subtle reasoning once he has grown old and impotent. But if someone attacked only evil women, and, as these men have done, advised against pursuing them, then some good could come of it. This — which is not to degrade all women indiscriminately — would be a reasonable act, a just, noble, and praiseworthy teaching. But let's speak for a moment of deceit. I simply cannot comprehend how a woman can deceive a man. She never pursues him, begging after him at his house; she doesn't give a thought to him, nor even remember him; whereas men come to deceive and entrap women. How does he tempt her? In truth, there is nothing that he will not endure gladly, no burden that he will not bear in order to have her. He devotes himself utterly to efforts to deceive her, even at the cost of his heart, his body, and his wealth. It often happens that this period of privation and suffering lasts a long time, even though, despite their best efforts, many fail in their pursuit. These are the men Ovid speaks about in his poem on the *Art of Love.* Out of the deep pity he felt for them, he composed a book to teach them how to trick women into bestowing their favors on them. He called it the *Art of Love,* but far from teaching the code and traditions of noble love, he teaches the exact opposite. For whoever seeks to learn from this book will never know how to love, however much he may be loved. So, this book is badly named: it is rather a book of the art of sheer deceit and dissimulation — that's the name I give it. Yet since women are so flighty, fickle, changeable, guileful, and unreliable, why do suitors have to use trickery to bring them down? And why — since clerks so describe them — don't women quickly give in to them, without all this need for skill and ingenuity in wooing them? There is no need to go to war for a castle that is already captured. Take, for example, a poet as skilful as Ovid, who was sent into exile, or Jean de Meun, in his *Roman de la Rose*. What a lengthy business! What a difficult task; What a mixture of clear and cloudy ideas, how many great adventures he puts in it! See how many men beg and plead, see what trouble and difficulties they undergo to undo a mere little girl by deceit and guile — this is its purpose. Does then a weak place need a heavy assault? How can one take a great leap, while standing so close to his mark? I simply cannot see or understand why it requires great effort to capture a weak place, what skill or ingenuity or great cunning is needed. Hence, since it does indeed require such skill, ingenuity, and effort to seduce a woman, either of high or humble birth, it is perfectly clear that women are not all as fickle or unpredictable in their conduct as some men claim. And if anyone tells me that books are full of women like these, this very reply is what causes me to complain. My answer is that women did not write these books, wherein can be read these slights on them and their morals. Those who plead their cause in the absence of an opponent can invent to their heart's content, can tell endless tales and keep the best parts for themselves, because aggressors have no qualms about attacking those who do not defend themselves. But if women had written these books, I know full well the matter would have been handled differently. They know that they stand wrongfully accused, and that the sharing has not been done evenly, for the strong take the biggest share, and the one who does the dividing keeps the biggest portion for himself. Yet malicious slanderers who debase women in this way still maintain that all women have been, are now, and always will be false, asserting that they have never been capable of loyalty. They say that lovers find all women to be like this when they approach them amorously. At every turn, women are put in the wrong: whatever wrong has been done is attributed to them. This is a damnable lie, and one can easily see that the contrary is true. For, in matters of love, far too many women have been, are now, and will be faithful, in spite of deceit and falsehoods, deception and trickery, and the numerous lies which have been used against them. [309-436]

… …

For this reason, I say no more; let everyone judge rightly according to the truth. If he does judge rightly, he will find that the greatest apparent evil may do little harm. Women kill no one, wound no one, torture no one; they are not treacherous; they set no fires, disinherit no one, poison no one, take neither gold nor silver, cheat no one out of his wealth or inheritance, make no false contracts, nor bring any harm to kingdoms, duchies, or empires. [641-651

II

TREATISE
OF
JEAN DE MONTREUIL
NOW LOST

[*In* Der Streit um den Rosenroman, *Peter Potansky gives a con-
jectured reconstruction of this document. By noting statements
and general argumentative stances taken alike by Christine de
Pisan in her first letter and Jean Gerson in his reply to Pierre
Col, and particularly wherein these two correspond closely to
one another, as they sometimes do to a striking degree, Potansky
has presented a strong case for reconstruction.*]

III

JEAN DE MONTREUIL
CUM UT DANT SESE RES

[This brief letter in crabbed and tortuous Latin was probably written at the beginning of the year 1401, and its recipient, Potansky believes, was Pierre d'Ailly. The Latin text can be found in Jean de Montreuil, Opera, *ed. Ezio Ornato (Torino: G. Giappichelli, 1963), I, 144-145, Letter 103].*

My most reverend father, Gontier [1] recently encouraged, indeed impelled me to read the *Roman de la Rose,* and I hastened to do so. Then in the French language I described the genius of the author [2] and how the book had borne up under severe attack, as your Reverence will see by the appended work. Yet lest I should seem to neglect my serious tasks by dabbling in trivia — indeed it is contrary to my calling to do such — I hasten to add that, as sometimes happens, nothing else was taking place to engage my attention at the time that I composed this work.

Therefore, my Lord, I am submitting it for you to decide whether I praised the author too much, too little, or with moderation, as well as to ask that you indicate to this adopted son of

---

[1] Gontier Col. This letter seems to indicate that the debate was, rather vehemently, in progress even before the discussions mentioned by Christine de Pisan.

[2] This is a reference, apparently, to Montreuil's famous lost treatise, which, as he makes clear, was written in French.

yours, as far as your higher tasks permit, whether a copy of my letter to our Lingonian Treasurer[3] sent out some days ago has come to the attention of your Lordship. Farewell and please approve. [145]

---

[3] *Lingonian Treasurer.* Potansky suggests that the person referred to is Nicholas de Clamanges.

IV

JEAN DE MONTREUIL
QUO MAGIS

[The earlier belief that the recipient of this letter was Gerson has been discounted, and recent scholarship has been reluctant to draw any conclusions with regard to the matter. The context of the letter identifies its recipient as a man closely associated with legal matters and the courts, and beyond this it is not safe to go. The letter was probably written in the first half of the year 1401. The Latin text can be found in Ornato, I, 177-178, Letter 118.]

O most wise man, the more thoroughly I examine the mysterious loftiness and the lofty mysteries of that profound book of famous memory by Master Jean de Meun, and the more diligently I consider the genius of that artist, the more deeply am I moved and provoked to wonder what inspiration or frame of mind led you to censure that same famous and knowledgeable author for having spoken too frivolously, scurrilously, and ineptly. I am surprised that you especially could do so, since you daily deal with civil suits which require to the highest degree serious and careful deliberation and sound judgment of delicate matters. Just day before yesterday as if arguing in the courtroom, you spoke against a dead man, and debated furiously; then, you expressed a far greater preference for Guillaume de Lorris on account of his originality, clarity, elegance, and precision. At that time moved by a certain consideration, I declined to respond to your attack, and still do so. But if you confess that you spoke seriously, tell me for what prize you contend; [1] I shall come, as Virgil said, whithersoever you have called. [2] I shall not desert my masters and benefactors until my dying breath, nor, while it is in my power, will I permit their honor to be besmirched. If on the contrary, as I rather suspect, you argued in jest, or perhaps were influenced by another person, we are not so severe that we do not appreciate the freedom of exchange permissible in debate or do not know how to be indulgent toward exchange of words. Indeed, since truth is discovered through debate, as gold is proved in the furnace, [3] I agree that certainly one can discuss the talent of this most ingenious teacher, provided that you assert nothing strongly and obstinately in the future against our disciple. [4]

Farewell, and with regard to this matter, let me know what you intend. For we make no secret of our intent, should you continue to speak ill of our teacher. Take this, as of now, for a challenge. There are indeed (may you not doubt it) many fighters and champions who will defend this cause to the limits of their power by writing, word, and deed alike.

[178]

---

[1] Vergil, *Bucolica,* III.31.
[2] Vergil, *Bucolica,* III.49.
[3] Proverbs, XXVII.21.
[4] Montreuil's Latin word is *imitatorem,* where thinking in terms of Jean de Meun, one might have expected *auctorem.* Montreuil, however, apparently has in mind some disciple of his, who had written in support of the *Roman de la Rose* and been harshly criticized for that fact.

V

JEAN DE MONTREUIL
ETSI FACUNDISSIMUS

*[This letter was apparently written only a short time after the
preceding one* (Quo magis) *and was addressed to the same unknown person. It is a reiteration and a strengthening of the
positions of the* Quo magis *letter. The Latin text is in Ornato,
I, 182-183, Letter 122.]*

Although you are most fluent, eloquent, articulate, and, O illus-
trious man, that which is the fountain of writing,[1] a wise man, yet
I see that, because of conquering truth and a biting conscience,
you dare not utter anything further[2] or build a case against that
exacting satirist, Master Jean de Meun. Indeed, the power of
that same truth is so great that no skillful rhetorician can match
it, for as the saying goes: "Truth remains forever;[3] false things
do not last."[4]

Reconcile yourself, therefore, with that same learned one and
most beloved teacher, and do not fear because you spoke rashly.
For immediately upon seeking our grace, you will receive it, as long
as we have no reservation concerning the sincerity of your pro-
fessed repentance. For we are, of course, aware how far the license

---

[1] Cf. Horace, *Ars poetica,* 309.
[2] Terence, *Andria,* 505.
[3] Ps. CXVI.2. For biblical quotations throughout, we have used the Douay-
Rheims version, as the closest to the Vulgate in English. In modern versions
the numbering of the Psalms is generally one number higher.
[4] Seneca, *Ad. Lucil.,* CXX.19.

of disputation extends and how often the early morning disputation contradicts the conclusions of the evening before. O learned man, you know, furthermore, that both Origen and Lactantius erred, and likewise that Augustine and many other learned and famous men have retracted. Therefore, one should not be ashamed to repair things said unrestrainedly and put forth in error. It may well be that you read those things you condemn carelessly and some time ago. It is these two factors which distorted your judgment and led you into precipitate error, not certainly an error of faith, nor even of deliberate wickedness, but one into which a good number of the supporters of Meun himself have rushed with you, for they too, in their haste, have only a shallow understanding of him. Do not consider our present admonition slight or believe it to be lacking in brotherly love. And do not think that in our previous friendly [182] correspondence I warned you idly about the admirers and defenders of the excellent philosopher. For there are champions with shining spurs, holders of high rank, who in order to protect our cause strive after beautiful death by combat, as Virgil says; [5] such men think nothing more pleasing to God than to assail those who condemn our mentor for a mere syllable or trivial detail. But you ask what to do. I exhort you to say that which the prophet and king did not blush humbly to confess: "I made known my crime to you, and my injustice I did not hide." [6] But if you should write a treatise on this subject in the meantime, I pray, in the name of our friendship, that it become in no way a source of pain for you to send to your provost [7] some kind of communication, which may serve above all to alleviate our uncertainty and to indicate in some way your intent. Then with the Psalmist, "I will rejoice over your eloquence like a man who has found great treasure." [8] Farewell.   [183]

---

[5] *Georgics,* IV.218; *Aeneid,* XI.647: "pulchramque petunt per vulnera mortem."

[6] Ps. XXXI.5.

[7] i.e. himself.

[8] Ps. CXVIII.162.

VI

CHRISTINE DE PISAN TO JEAN DE MONTREUIL

[This letter, Christine's first entry in the debate proper, was written some time in the middle of the year 1401, certainly before September 13, when Gontier Col wrote Christine for the first time asking for a copy of her letter. Christine here answers a letter of Montreuil's, which, although not specifically addressed to her, did deal with matters that she was very much aware of from previous discussions (as we learn from her own remarks; see page 68), as well as from the fact that Montreuil saw fit to send her a copy of the letter. The Old French text is in The Epistles on the Romance of the Rose and Other Documents in the Debate, *ed. Charles Frederick Ward (Chicago, 1911), pp. 17-28.]*

To the very competent and wise person, Master John,[1] Secretary of the King our Lord and Provost of Lisle.

Reverence, honor, and due respect to you, Lord Provost of Lisle, esteemed Master, sage in morals, lover of knowledge, steeped in learning, and expert in rhetoric; from me, Christine de Pisan, a woman weak in understanding and inadequate in learning — for which things may your sagacity not hold in scorn the smallness of my reasons; rather may it take into account my feminine weakness. It has pleased you out of your goodness (for which I say thanks) to send me a small treatise expressed in fine language and true-seeming reasons. Your treatise was written, as I gather from your

---

[1] Christine writes "Jehan Johannes," which was a frequent designation for Jean de Montreuil.

own words, to oppose critics of certain parts of the *Roman de la Rose,* to give firm support to the work, and to approve it and its authors, and in particular Meun. Having read and considered your letter and having understood it, within the limits of my ability, I disagreed with your remarks and shared the opinion of the learned man to whom your letter was addressed. Therefore, although your letter was not addressed to me and did not require a reply, nevertheless I wish to say, to divulge, and to maintain openly that (saving your good grace) you are in grave error to give such lavish and unjustified praise to Meun's book — one which could better be called plain idleness [2] than useful work, in my judgment. You severely criticize his opponents and say, "that a great thing is therein to be understood," "that what a third party says gives a better testimony," "has constructed and erected through great study and at great length." [3] Yet may my daring to repudiate and find fault with an author so worthy and so subtle not seem presumption in me. Rather, take heed of the firm conviction which has moved me to oppose some opinions contained in your letter. In truth, a [17] mere assertion not justified by law can be re-argued without prejudice. I am not, I confess, learned nor schooled in the subtle language, which would make my arguments dazzling, a language which you indeed can display with a fine array of carefully polished words. Nevertheless, I will not hesitate to express my opinion bluntly in the vernacular, although I may not be able to express myself elegantly.

But why did I say before that Meun's work could best be called idleness? Certainly, it seems to me that any trivial thing, even though it is treated, composed, and accomplished with great labor and difficulty, can be called idle, or worse than idle, insofar as evil follows from it. Yet because of the great and widespread fame of the said romance, I had long desired to read it, and once I had gained the knowledge to understand subtle matters somewhat, I did read and consider it at length, to the best of my ability. It is

---

[2] Christine's word here is *oisiueté.* Is this not a half-amused allusion to Lady *Oiseuse,* keeper of the wicket gate of the garden in the *Roman de la Rose.* Not only is the garden to be condemned, *because* it is kept by Lady Idleness (see Gerson's argument, p. 88), but also the entire romance, which, for all the effort and industry that went into it, is mere trifling "idleness."

[3] These few fragments are all that remain of Montreuil's treatise.

true that the subject matter did not please me in certain parts and so I skipped over it as quickly as a cock over hot embers; therefore, I have not read it in every detail. Nevertheless, some things have remained in my memory which my judgment strongly condemned, and still cannot approve, despite the contrary praise of other people. It is quite true that my small understanding finds great prettiness there; in some parts, he expresses himself very well indeed, using beautiful terms and graceful leonine rhyme. He could not have treated his subject more subtly or more skilfully. But I agree with the opinion (which you clearly oppose, it seems to me) that he speaks too dishonorably in some parts of the *Roman de la Rose,* even when he speaks through the character he calls Reason, who names the secret members plainly by name. [4] You, in fact, support Meun and say that such frankness is perfectly reasonable, maintaining that in the things God has made there is no ugliness, and consequently no need to eschew their names. To this I say and confess that truly God created all things pure and clean coming [18] from himself and that in the State of Innocence it would not have been wrong to name them; but by the pollution of sin man became impure, and his original sin has remained with us, as Holy Scripture testifies. I can make this clear by a comparison: God made Lucifer beautiful above all the angels and gave him a very solemn and beautiful name, but then Lucifer was reduced by his sin to horrible ugliness; whereupon, the name, albeit very beautiful in itself, now, because of the impression of the person, creates horror in those who hear it.

Further, you point out that Jesus Christ calls the women sinners *meretrix,* [5] etc. But I can explain to you why he called them by that name, because the name *meretrix* is not particularly dishonorable to utter considering the vileness of the thing named, and, in fact, it could have been more basely said even in Latin. Thus should modesty be respected when speaking publicly of things about which Nature herself is ashamed. Saving your reverence and the author's, I say that you commit great wrong against the noble

---

[4] See *Le Roman de la Rose,* ed. Ernest Langlois, SATF 63 (1914; rpt. New York: Johnson Reprint Corporation, 1965), lines 5537 and 6943-48. Further references to the *Roman de la Rose* will be to this edition.

[5] See Matthew XXI.31-32; Luke XV.30.

virtue of modesty, which by its nature bridles indecency and dishonorable conduct in words and deeds. Holy Scripture makes clear in many places that this is a great wrong, outside the range of decent conduct and good morals. Moreover, I affirm that the indecent name should not be avoided by substituting the word "relics" for it. [6] I suggest to you that the name does not make the thing dishonorable, but the thing, the name. Therefore, in my humble opinion, one should speak about such matters soberly and only when necessary, as in certain particular cases, such as sickness or other genuine need. Just as our first parents hid their private parts instinctively, so ought we to do in deed and in word.

Further, I cannot be silent about a subject that so displeases me: that the function of Reason, whom he even calls the daughter of God, should be to propound such a dictum as the one I found in the chapter where Reason says to the Lover, "In the amorous war, it is better to deceive than to be deceived." [7] And truly, Master Jean de Meun, I dare say that Reason denied her heavenly father in that teaching, for He taught an utterly different doctrine. If you hold one of these two to be better than the other, it would follow that both are good, and this cannot be. I hold a contrary opinion: it is far less evil, clearly, to be deceived than to deceive.   [19]

Further, let us consider the subject matter or choice of words, which many people find reprehensible. Dear Lord! What horrible stuff! What an affront to honor! What reprehensible teachings recorded in the chapter about the Old Woman! [8] In God's name, what can one find there but sophistical exhortations filled with ugliness and things horrible to recall? Ha, you who have beautiful daughters! If you really want to introduce them to the honorable life, give them, give them, I say, this book so that they may learn from the *Roman de la Rose* ways to distinguish Good from Evil — what am I saying! — rather Evil from Good! To what purpose or to what profit is it that the hearers of this book have their ears assailed by so much sinfulness?

Then, in the chapter about Jealousy, [9] my God, what great good can be observed there! What need to record the dishonorable things

---

[6] See *Roman de la Rose,* 21583-602.
[7] Lines 4399-4400.
[8] Lines 12385-14546.
[9] Lines 8455-9492.

and the shameful words, which are common enough in the mouths
of the unfortunate people impassioned by this sickness! What good
example or preparation for life could this be? And the wickedness
which is there recorded of women! Many people attempt to excuse
him by saying that it is the Jealous Man who speaks and that in
truth Meun does no more than God himself did when He spoke
through the mouth of Jeremiah! But whatever lying additions he
may have made, he certainly could not have rendered worse or
abased the condition of women more! Ha! When I remember the
deceits, the hypocrisies, and the conduct dissembled within marriage
and outside it, which one can find in this book — certainly, I consider these to be beautiful and edifying tales for one to hear!

Further, what great marvels does the character that he calls
Genius the priest say! Surely, the works of Nature would have
completely fallen into disuse long since, if he had not so greatly
recommended them! But, my God, who could show or convince
me what profit there is in the great argument full of vituperation
that he calls a sermon (as if to deride holy preaching), which, he   [20]
says, Genius delivers? [10] It contains too many dishonorable things,
names, sophistical words, fanning the flames of those secrets of
Nature which ought to be left tacit and not named. Moreover, the
"sermon" is superfluous, for a work which is of the very order of
Nature cannot, obviously, fail. If it were not so, then it would be
good for the maintenance of human generation to invent and say
exciting and inflaming words and terms in order to stimulate man
to continue that work.

Yet the author does more, if I remember well; for the life of
me I can't understand to what purpose. For in the said sermon
he adduces, as a comparison, paradise and its joys. [11] He says truly
enough that the virtuous will go to that place, but he concludes
that everyone, men and women alike, should know how to perform
and exercise the functions of Nature; nor in this does he make any
exception of law, as if he wished to say, and indeed says plainly,
that they will all be saved. And by this it appears that he wishes
to maintain that the sin of lechery is nothing, rather a virtue,
which is error and against the law of God. Ha! what seed and

---

[10] See lines 19505-20667.
[11] Lines 19931-20036.

what doctrine! What great good can come of it! I believe that
many have left the world because of it and entered religion, or
become hermits because of that holy message, or come out of the
evil life and been saved by such exhortation! Certainly (I dare say
it, no matter whom it offends), this never came from anywhere
but a heart corrupted and abandoned to dissolution and vice, which
can be cause of great sin and unbecoming conduct.   [21]

And again, for God's sake, let us look a little further to see
what profit there can possibly be in his excessive, impetuous, and
most untruthful criticism and denigration of women as exceedingly
wicked creatures! He declares that their conduct is filled with all
manner of perversity, with which condemnations, even with all the
give and take among his characters, he cannot fully gorge himself.
For if you wish to tell me that the Jealous Man does this as a man
overcome by passion, I fail to see how he fulfills the teaching of
Genius, for Genius so fully recommends and exhorts men to bed
them and to perform the act which he praises so highly. And this
Genius, more than any of the characters, makes great attacks on
women, saying, in fact, "Flee, flee, flee from the deadly serpent." [12]
Then he declares that men should pursue them unremittingly. Here
is a glaring contradiction, evilly intended: to order men to flee
what he wishes them to pursue, and to pursue what he wishes them
to flee. But since women are so perverse, he ought not to command
men to approach them at all. For he who fears a problem ought
to eschew it. And it is for this reason that he so strongly forbids
a man to tell his secret to a woman, who is so eager to know it
(as he records), although I simply do not know where the devil he
found so much nonsense and so many useless words, which are
there laid out by a long process. But I pray all those who truly
hold this teaching authentic and put so much faith in it, that they
kindly tell me how many men they have seen accused, killed,
hanged, and publicly rebuked by the accusations of their women?
I think you will find them few and far between. Nevertheless, it   [22]
would be good and praiseworthy counsel for a man to keep his
affairs to himself for the greatest security, for he who does so is
rich above all men. Indeed, not long ago I heard tell of a man who

---

[12] See lines 16586-92. Cf. Vergil, *Bucolica*, III.92-93.

was accused and hanged on account of having revealed himself to
a friend whom he trusted. But I think that few have come before a
judge with accusations or complaints of such horrible evil, such
disloyalties, and such wickedness which he says women know how
to commit so maliciously and underhandedly. It is indeed secret
when nobody sees it. As I have said previously on this subject in
my work called "L'Epistre au Dieu d'Amours," where are those
countries and kingdoms which have been ruined by the great evils
of women? If it be not presumptuous, let us speak of the great
crimes that one can attribute to even the worst and most deceitful
of women. What do they do? In what ways do they deceive you?
If they ask you for money from your purse, which they cannot get
from you by a ruse or cannot take themselves, do not give it to
them if you do not wish to. And if you say that they have made
a fool of you, don't let them. Do they go into your house to woo,
pursue, or rape you? It would be good to know how they deceive you. And, besides, he speaks superficially and wrongly about
married women who deceive their husbands in this way, for he
could know nothing of the married state by experience, and therefore he spoke of it only in generalities. I do not understand what
good purpose this can serve or what good can come of it, save to
impede the good and peace that is in marriage, and to render the
husbands who hear so much babbling and extravagance (if they
believe such things) suspicious and less affectionate toward their
wives. God, what exhortation! How profitable it is! But truly since
he blamed all women in general, I am constrained to believe that he
never had acquaintance of, or regular contact with, any honorable
or virtuous woman. But by having resort to many dissolute women
of evil life (as lechers commonly do), he thought, or feigned to   [23]
know, that all women were of that kind; for he had known no
others. And if he had blamed only the dishonorable ones and coun-
seled men to flee them, it would have been a good and just teaching. But no, without exception he accuses them all. But if, beyond
all the bounds of reason, the author took it upon himself to accuse
or judge them without justification, the ones accused ought not to
be blamed for it. Rather, he should be blamed who carried his
argument to the point where it was simply not true, since the
contrary is so obvious. For if he and all his henchmen had sworn
it in this matter (let no one take offense), there have been, there

are, and there will be more virtuous women, more honorable, better bred, and even more learned, and from whom more great good has come forth into the world than ever did from his person. Similarly, there have been women well schooled in worldly conduct and virtuous morals, and many who have effected a reconciliation with their husbands and have borne their concerns and their secrets and their passions calmly and discreetly, despite the fact that their husbands were crude and brutish toward them. One finds proof enough of this in the Bible and in other ancient histories, women such as Sarah, Rebeccah, Esther, Judith, and many others. And even in our own time we have seen in France many virtuous women, great ladies and others of our ladies of France: the holy devout Queen Jeanne; Queen Blanche; the Duchess of Orliens, daughter of the King of France; the Duchess of Anjou, who is now called Queen of Sicily; and many others — all of whom had such great beauty, chastity, honor, and wisdom. And also women of lesser rank, like Madame de la Ferté, wife of Monsieur Pierre de Craon, [24] who did much that was praiseworthy; besides many others, whom I pass over for lack of time.

And do not believe or let anyone else think, dear Sir, that I have written this defense, out of feminine bias, merely because I am a woman. For, assuredly, my motive is simply to uphold the pure truth, since I know by experience that the truth is completely contrary to those things I am denying. And it is precisely because I am a woman that I can speak better in this matter than one who has not had the experience, since he speaks only by conjecture and by chance. But above all these things, pray let us consider what the aim of the aforementioned treatise is; for as the proverb says, "By the intent a case is concluded." Thus may be seen and noted what can be profitable in that excessively horrible and shameful conclusion.[13] I call it shameful and so very dishonorable that I dare say that nobody who loves virtue and honor will hear it without being totally confounded by shame and abomination at hearing described, expressed, and distorted in dishonorable fictions what modesty and reason should restrain well-bred folk from even thinking about. Yet, further, I dare say that even the goliards would

---

[13] Christine refers here, of course, to the thinly veiled description of the sexual act which concludes the *Roman de la Rose.*

have been horrified to read or hear it in public, in decent places, and before people whom they would have considered virtuous. But who could praise a work which can be neither read nor quoted at the table of queens, of princesses, and of worthy women, who would surely, on hearing it, be constrained to cover their blushing faces?

And if you wish to excuse him by saying that by means of a pretty novelty it pleases him to put the purpose of love through such figures, I answer you that in this work he tells us nothing   [25] new. Does one not know how men normally behave with women? If he had told us something about bears or lions or birds or other strange creatures, this would have been matter for laughing on account of the fable, but there is no novelty in this that he tells us. And certainly it could have been done more pleasantly, far more agreeably, and by means of more courteous terms, a method which would have been more pleasing to handsome and decent lovers and to every other virtuous person.

Thus, without being more prolix, although a great deal more could be said, and said better, I do not know how, according to my small capacity and weak judgment, to consider this book useful in any way. But it seems so very manifest to me that a great labor was expended on it which produced nothing of value, although my judgment concedes that Master Jean de Meun was a very great, learned, and eloquent clerk. But he would have been able to produce so much better a work, more profitable, and of higher sentiment, if he had applied himself to it, and that he did not do so is great loss. I suppose, however, that perhaps the great carnality with which he was filled caused him to abandon himself to desire rather than to the good of his soul, for by one's actions generally the inclinations are known. Notwithstanding, I do not condemn the *Roman de la Rose* entirely, for it does indeed contain some good things, and its style is poetically pleasing, but therein lies the greater peril, for the more authentic the good the more faith one puts in the evil. And in this way many learned men have sometimes sown great errors by intermingling good and evil and by covering the errors over with truth and virtue. Thus if his priest Genius can say, "Flee, flee woman, the evil serpent hidden in the grass"; I   [26] can say, "Flee, flee the malice concealed in the shadow of goodness and virtue."

Therefore, I say this in conclusion to you, dear Sir, and to all your allies who praise this work so highly and make so much of it that you dare and presume to minimize almost all other works by comparison — I say that it does not merit such praise (saving your good grace) and that you do great wrong to the more deserving works. For a work without usefulness, contributing nothing to the general or personal good (even though we concede it to be delightful, the fruit of great work and labor), in no way deserves praise. And as in former times the triumphant Romans would not attribute praise or honor to anything if it was not to the utility of the Republic, let us look to their example to see whether we can crown this Romance. But having considered the aforementioned things and numerous others we have touched on, I consider it more fitting to bury it in fire than to crown it with laurel, although you call it a mirror of good living and, for men of all classes, an example of good social conduct and of the wise, moral life. But to the contrary (saving your grace) I call it an exhortation to vice, a comfort to dissolute life, a doctrine full of deception, the way to damnation, a public defamer, the cause of suspicion and misbelieving, the shame of many people, and possibly the occasion of heresy. But I know well that you will excuse it by replying to me that therein he enjoins man to do the good but to eschew the evil. But my reasoning is better, for I can show that there is no point in reminding human nature, which is naturally inclined to evil, that it limps on one foot, in the hope that it will then walk straighter. Do you wish to speak of all the good which can be found in this book? Certainly, far more virtuous things, eloquently expressed, closer to the truth, and more profitable to the decorous and moral life can be found in many other books — books written by certain philosophers and by teachers of our faith, like Aristotle, Seneca, St. Paul, St. Augustine, and others, as you well know. For these testify and teach how to pursue virtue and flee vice more clearly and plainly than Master Jean de Meun has ever been able to do. But such teachings are not usually heard or remembered by fleshly men. They are like the thirsty invalid who, when the doctor permits him to drink, does so gladly and excessively, for the lust for drink-

[27]

ing leads him to believe that now it will do him no harm.[14] If by God's grace you were restored to the light and purity of a clear conscience, freed from the stain and pollution of sin or any sinful intent, and purged by the prick of contrition which reveals the secrets of conscience and condemns self-will — and may God grant it to you and to all others — then you would be more receptive to truth and thus would make a different judgment of the *Rose*; perhaps you would wish that you had never seen it. So much suffices. And may it not be imputed to me as folly, arrogance, or presumption, that I, a woman, should dare to reproach and call into question so subtle an author, and to diminish the stature of his work, when he alone, a man, has dared to undertake to defame and blame without exception an entire sex.   [28]

---

[14] The passage is somewhat difficult to translate, because the comparison contains only its first term and is not completely worked out. Cf. Ovid, *Amores,* III.iv.18.

VII

GONTIER COL TO CHRISTINE DE PISAN

*[Containing the unequivocal date of September 13, 1401, this brief
letter is essentially a declaration of support for Jean de Meun,
that "worthy master," and a request by Gontier Col for a copy
of Christine's letter to Jean de Montreuil, which he has heard
about. The Old French text is in Ward, pp. 29-30.]*

To the worthy, honored, and wise damoiselle Christine:

Woman of high and exalted understanding, worthy of honor
and great esteem, I have heard say from many notable clerks that
among your other studies and virtuous and praiseworthy works, as
I understand by their remarks, you have recently written a kind
of invective against the book of the *Rose* composed by my master,
teacher, and friend, the lamented Master Jean de Meun, true Catholic, worthy master, and, in his time, doctor of holy theology, a
most profound and excellent philosopher, knowing all that to human
understanding is knowable, whose glory and fame lives and will
live in the ages to come among understanding men, elevated by his
merits, by the grace of God, and by the work of Nature. According
to those who have made this report, you expend great effort to
charge him with faults in your work, and this fact makes me wonder
and marvel exceedingly. My incredulity arises from my own personal
knowledge of you, as well as from the fact that I have read and
fully understood him in the abovementioned book and in his other
works written in French, not to mention other teachers, authors,
and poets. Yet those who condemn Jean de Meun (some perhaps
out of pure envy) regard your invective as a remarkably well

designed argument. And since the work was written solely to please and support them, I am unable to get either a copy or the original from them. Therefore, I beg and pray, on the love you have for knowledge, that you send me by this messenger, or by another if you like, an exact copy of your work. I wish to have it in hand so that I can support and defend my master and his work. Yet there would have been no need for me or for any mortal to involve himself in the quarrel if Meun were now alive. Oh, that he were living now! This would make me happier than to be Emperor of Rome.

To bring you back to the real truth and to help you to know and understand the works of the said Meun better, I am sending you, in good faith and promptly, a little treasure[1] which Meun wrote, to be made known to his detractors and others upon his death. This treasure may indeed give you material for more writings against him if that appeals to you, or to your satellites. They, in fact, were the ones who pushed you into this affair, because they did not dare, or rather did not know how, to handle such a matter, but wanted to use you as their cloak, to imply that they knew more about the matter than a woman and thereby further to diminish the reputation, already undervalued by mortals, of such a man. This book which I am sending is incorrect through fault of the scribe, who apparently did not understand it. I, for my part, have not had the time or leisure to inspect or correct it at length, because of my urgent desire to see your work. Besides, one can suppose that you will be able to recognize and amend the scribe's errors in this book. But with regard to what Meun did with the book of the *Rose,* which is far longer and more complex, you have chosen, nay dared, to accuse him, correct him, and criticize him. But there's one thing I do not wish to forget or gloss over: although I am at present engaged in other serious tasks and have been recently, I will undertake to support him against any of your writings whatsoever, unless you withdraw or retract, for I am confident of good and true justice and certain that truth, which proceeds directly,[2] will be on my side.

[29]

---

[1] A punning reference to *Le Tresor de maistre Jehan de Meung ou les Septs Articles de la Foi.*

[2] The text reads "vérité (qui ne quiert angles)." Cf. St. Jerome in the letter to Rusticus, "Veritas angulos non amat nec quaerit susurrones." See

Written hastily in the presence of Messrs. John de Quatre Mares and John Porchier, counselors, and Guillaume de Neauville, secretary of the King our lord, Tuesday, the 13th of Sept., 1401.

Yours, within the bounds of friendship — Gontier Col,

Secretary of the King our Lord. [30]

Select Letters of St. Jerome, trans. F. A. Wright (Cambridge, Mass.: Harvard University Press, 1963), Letter CXXV, pp. 434-435.

VIII

GONTIER COL TO CHRISTINE DE PISAN

*[Written two days after the preceding one, that is, September 15,
1401, this letter is apparently Gontier Col's first angry response
to Christine's letter to Montreuil. The Old French text is avail-
able in Ward, pp. 30-31.]*

Holy Scripture teaches and commands us that when someone
sees his friend err or do wrong, he ought first of all to correct and
reproach him in private, and if thereafter he will not amend himself, that one ought to correct him in public, and if even so he will
not mend his ways, that one should hold him as *ethnicus* or *publi-* [30]
canus. [1] Therefore, since I love you sincerely for your virtues and
merits, I have first by my letter (which I sent to you day before
yesterday) exhorted, advised, and begged you to correct and amend
your manifest error, folly, or excessive wilfulness which has risen
in you, a woman impassioned in this matter, out of presumption
or arrogance — may it not displease you if I speak the truth. Thus
following the holy commandment and having compassion for you
by charitable love, I pray, counsel, and require you a second time
by this little note of mine please to correct, retract, and amend
your aforementioned error with regard to that very excellent and
irreproachable doctor of holy divine Scripture, high philosopher,
and most learned clerk in all the seven liberal arts. It is astonishing

---

[1] See Matthew XVIII.15-17. For our "ethicus" in this sentence, the MSS.
read "eunucus." Beck suggested the emendation. See F. Beck, *Les Epistres sur
le Roman de la Rose von Christine de Pizan nach drei Pariser Hss. bearbeitet
und zum ersten Mal veröffentlicht* (Neuberg, 1888).

that you have dared and presumed to correct and criticize him detrimentally, as well as his true and loyal disciples: Monsieur the Provost of Lisle and me and others. Confess your error, and we will have pity on you, will grant mercy to you, and will give you salutary penance. And concerning this matter, in your reply to my other letter kindly let me know at your convenience what your wishes are, before I take the trouble to oppose the false (saving your reverence) judgments which you have seen fit to write against him. And if now and henceforth when I write to you I make use of the singular pronoun, please do not be offended; and do not think it arrogance or pride in me, for it is and always has been my custom when I write to my friends, especially when they are learned. May it please God soon to bring your heart and understanding back to the true light and knowledge of truth, for it would be a great pity if you should remain longer in such error under the darkness of ignorance. Written Thursday, 15th day of September.

Yours,   Gontier Col.   [31]

IX

CHRISTINE DE PISAN TO GONTIER COL

*[This letter, as its context makes clear, was written some time
after the two preceding ones, and is in answer to them. A date
in October 1401, as Potansky suggests, is safe enough. The
Old French text is in Ward, pp. 32-33.]*

To the most noble and excellent person, Master Gontier Col,
Secretary of the King our Lord:

O wise clerk of philosophic mind, knowledgeable, and accomplished in polished rhetoric and poetic subtlety, please do not
willfully choose to reproach and reprove my true opinion, honestly
arrived at, just because it is not to your pleasure. I learned from
your first letter that you desire to have a copy of a little epistolary
treatise which I had previously sent to the worthy clerk, Monsei-
gneur the Provost of Lisle. In this treatise I discussed at length
(within the limitations of my small wit) my views, which differed
so greatly from the praise which he lavished on the *Roman de la
Rose,* expressed, so I discovered, in a letter to a friend of his, a
wise and learned clerk. This praise was completely contrary to the
opinion of his friend, with whom I agreed. And so in order to meet
your wishes, I sent the letter requested. Whereupon, after you had
read and thoroughly scrutinized my letter, wherein your error was
punctured by truth, you wrote in a fit of impatience your second,
more offensive letter, reproaching my feminine sex, which you
describe as impassioned by nature. Thus you accuse me, a woman,
of folly and presumption in daring to correct and reproach a teacher
as exalted, well-qualified, and worthy as you claim the author of

that book to be. Hence, you earnestly exhort me to recant and repent. Whereupon, you say, generous mercy will still be extended to me, but that, if not, I shall be treated as a publican, etc. Ha! man of ingenious understanding! Don't let your own wilfulness blunt the acuity of your mind! Look rightly according to the most sovereign theological way, and, far from condemning what I have written, you will ask yourself whether one ought to praise those particular passages I have condemned. And, furthermore, note everywhere carefully which things I condemn and which I do not. And if you despise my reasons so much because of the inadequacy of my faculties, which you criticize by your words, "a woman impassioned," etc., rest assured that I do not feel any sting in such criticism, thanks to the comfort I find in the knowledge that there are, and have been, vast numbers of excellent, praiseworthy women, schooled in all the virtues — whom *I* would rather resemble than to be enriched with all the goods of fortune.[1] But, further, if you seek in every way to minimize my firm beliefs by your anti-feminist attacks, please recall that a small dagger or knife point can pierce a great, bulging sack and that a small fly can attack a great lion and speedily put him to flight. So, although by speaking evil of me you seek to threaten me with your subtle reasoning, which is commonly a source of fear to the faint-hearted, do not imagine me so moved or carried away by flightiness that I can be quickly defeated. Therefore, so that you may retain in brief what I have at other times written at length, I say again and repeat and repeat again as many times as you wish my condemnation of the work entitled the *Roman de la Rose*. I say that it can be a source of wicked and perverse encouragement to disgusting conduct, although it does contain some good things (the more authentic the good, the greater the evil, as I have said before), because mankind is naturally inclined to evil. This book can be, for many people, a supporter of the dissolute life; a doctrine full of deceit; the road to damnation; a public defamer; a source of suspicion, mistrust, shame, and, perhaps, of heresy. And in several places a most loathsome book!

[32]

---

[1] This appears to be a clear and intentional echo of Gontier Col's similar remark in his first letter.

All this I choose and dare to hold and maintain everywhere and before everyone, and I can prove it by reference to the book itself. I expect and rely on the favorable judgment of all just men, theologians, true Catholics, and people of honorable and good life.

Yours,   Christine de Pisan   [33]

X

CHRISTINE DE PISAN'S DEDICATORY LETTER
TO THE QUEEN OF FRANCE

*[This letter, as well as the following one to Tignonville, was
written to accompany and introduce a collection of the documents in the debate to that point. Although we have no indication of the outcome of such a bold move, the action itself
denotes a very much aware and politically sensitive individual.
The letter is dated February 1, 1401. The Old French text is
in Ward, pp. 34-35.]*

To the most noble, exalted, and awesome Princess, Madame Isabeau
of Bavaria, by the grace of God Queen of France.

Most exalted, most powerful, and most awesome Lady, accept
my humble esteem above all. I have heard that your Excellency
delights to hear virtuous and well-expressed works, a laudable
practice which increases virtue and good morals for your noble
person. For as a wise man said: "Virtue added to virtue, and
wisdom to nobility make that person worthy, who can already be
considered perfect." And my awesome Lady, because such virtue is
found in your noble understanding, it is fitting that works on
selected subjects should be presented to you as sovereign. Although
I am very simple and ignorant among women, your humble cham-
bermaid, subject to you, eager to serve you (if you consider me
worthy), I am moved to send you the present letters. In these
letters, my most awesome Lady, if you deign to honor me by
listening to them, you can understand my diligence, desire, and
wish to resist by true defenses, as far as my small power extends,

some false opinions denigrating the honor and fair name of women, which many men — clerks and others — have striven to diminish by their writings. This is a thing not to be permitted, suffered, or [34] supported. Although I am weak to lead the attack against such subtle masters, nonetheless my small wit has chosen and now chooses to employ itself in disputing those who attack and accuse women, for, being moved by the truth, I am firmly convinced that the feminine cause is worthy of defence. This I do here and have done in my other works. Thus, your worthy Highness, I petition humbly that you accept my argument, although I cannot express it in as fine a language as another might, and permit me to enlarge upon it, if, in the future, I am able to. May all this be done under your wise and benign correction. Most high and excellent, my most awe-inspiring Lady, I pray the True Trinity that you be granted a long and goodly life and fulfillment of all your desires.

Written the Eve of Candlemas the year 1401.
Your most humble creature,
Christine de Pisan   [35]

XI

CHRISTINE DE PISAN'S DEDICATORY LETTER
TO GUILLAUME DE TIGNONVILLE

*[Written, like the previous letter, on February 1, 1401, to ac-
company a collection of the documents, this letter asks support
from Guillaume de Tignonville, the powerful provost of Paris.
The Old French text is in Ward, pp. 35-36.]*

To my very dear Lord, noble and wise knight, Messire Guillaume
de Tignonville, Provost of Paris.

My Lord Provost of Paris, placed in so worthy a position and
office as guardian of high justice by the grace of God and your
own wisdom, accept esteem and obedience from me, Christine de
Pisan, weak of understanding and least among women desiring
honorable life. I write to inform you that, confident of your sagacity and worth, I am moved to call your attention to the good-
humored debate stimulated by a difference of opinion among worthy
persons, namely, Master Gontier Col, at present General Counselor
of the King our Lord, and Master John, Provost of Lisle and
Secretary of the said Lord. You will be able to understand the
grounds of this debate by the letters we have exchanged and by
the references to it which follow hereinafter. In this matter, most
wise provost, I ask that you favor me by giving a hearing to the
facts of our debate, despite your laborious involvement in more
important and necessary tasks. And in this letter I request the
favorable and discreet exercise of your wisdom so that you consider
and rightly choose the cause which I favor, although I do not know
how to explain it vividly or put it in terms consonant and pro-

XII

THE TREATISE OF GERSON AGAINST THE
ROMAN DE LA ROSE

*[Although not a part of the epistolary debate as such, this doc-
ument, in the form of a literary allegorical débat, is eminently
a part of the Querelle as a whole, since it attacks earlier arguments in favor of the Roman de la Rose and, afterwards,
itself was the object of attack by Pierre Col and of support by
Christine de Pisan. The Treatise, or Vision as it was also called,
supplies its own date of May 18, 1402. Ward's Latin text is
not authentic, having been early translated from Old French,
apparently by someone other than Gerson and indeed by someone who was not at ease with French. The text is to be found
in Ernest Langlois, "Le Traité de Gerson contre le Roman de
la Rose," Romania, 45 (1919), 23-48.]*

On a certain early morning a little before my agile heart had
fully awakened, I had the impression that it flew on the feathered
wings of various thoughts to and fro, all the way to the true Court
of holy Christianity. Canonical Justice, defender of the law, was
there, sitting upon the throne of righteousness, sustained on the
one hand by Mercy, on the other by Truth. In her right hand
Justice held the scepter of reward; in her left, the keen sword of
punishment. She had vivacious and honorable eyes, more brilliant
than the morning star, yea truly than the sun itself. Her retinue
was a beautiful group: on her one side was the most wise Court,
and all round about her were her noble retainers, an army and a
barony of all the virtues. These are the true daughters of God and

[29]

of Free Will, namely Divine Love, Fortitude, Temperance, Humility, and others in great number. Sound Judgment was the chief and chancellor of the Court, joined in a firm companionship with wise Lady Reason. His secretaries were Prudence and Knowledge. Good Christian Faith and divine, celestial Wisdom were part of this small council. As aides to them were Memory, Providence, Good Sense, and many others. Theological Eloquence, who was moderate and temperate of speech, acted as Advocate for the Court. The promoter of law-suits was called Conscience, for there is nothing that she does not know and report.

Thus while I was delighting in the sight of all the beautiful order of this Court of Christianity and of Justice, the defender of right, it seemed to me that Conscience rose to her feet. She was responsible for presenting cases to the Court, along with Equity, who held the office of Master of Requests. Conscience held many petitions in her hand and in her breast. Among them there was one particular case (which I recall word for word) that contained the pitiful complaint of the most beautiful and most pure Chastity, who would never stoop to give thought to anything base or impure.

To Justice the law giver, who holds the place of God on earth, and to the universal Court of his devout and most Christian religion, Chastity, your faithful subject, humbly supplicates and requests that you provide a remedy and a brief warning against the intolerable deeds which a certain Foolish Lover has been doing and continues to do to me. And these are the Articles.

Article 1

This Foolish Lover seizes every chance to drive me, who am innocent, from the earth, and with me my good attendants: Modesty, Fear, and Dangier, the good door-keeper. None of them would either dare or deign to grant a single shameful kiss, a shameless look, a come-hither smile, or a frivolous word. And the Foolish Lover does this through an accursed Old Woman worse than the devil, who teaches, shows, and exhorts all young virgins to sell their bodies quickly and dearly without fear or shame. Nor should they, she holds, put a high premium on deceiving or forswearing, provided always that they gain something thereby. Neither need they hesitate at all before abandoning themselves, quickly while they are still

[30]

beautiful, to every dishonor and to carnal filth, whether with clerics or laymen or priests, without any discrimination.

Article 2

He wishes to forbid and condemn marriage, without exception by means of a suspicious, hateful, and evil-minded Jealous Man, both through his own words and those of my adversaries. And he enjoins men to hang or drown themselves, or to commit sins which ought not to be named, rather than to marry. And he reviles all women, without any exception, and renders them so hateful to all men that none would wish to take them in the bonds of matrimony.

Article 3

He castigates young men who have given themselves to religion, because, as he says, they are striving to lay aside their nature, and this thing is prejudice against me, for I am especially dedicated to religion.

Article 4

He throws everywhere a fire more burning and more foul than Greek Fire or sulphur. He throws, I say, the fire of lecherous words, impure and prohibited, sometimes in the name of Venus and Cupid or Genius, more often in his own name, through which burn and are consumed my beautiful home and habitations, my sacred temples of human souls; and I am most shamefully cast down.

Article 5

He slanders Lady Reason, my good Mistress, by imputing to her the madness and wicked blasphemy of encouraging people to speak bluntly, openly, and basely about everything, however abominable or shameful, even to people already dissolute and enemies of mine. Alas, if he did not wish to spare me, what wrong has Reason ever done against him? But that's the way it is. Indeed, he makes war against all the virtues.

ARTICLE 6

When he speaks of holy, divine, and spiritual things, he immediately mixes in the most dissolute words, in order to incite to every impurity. However, impurity shall not enter into that Paradise, which he himself describes. [31]

ARTICLE 7

He promises Paradise, glory, and reward to all men and women who perform the works of the flesh, even outside marriage. For in his own person and by his own examples, he counsels men to try out all kinds of women indiscriminately; and he slanders all those who would not do so, at least all those who cherish and revere me.

ARTICLE 8

In his own person, he uses holy and sacred words to name the dishonorable parts of the body and impure and shameful sins, as if all such works were divine, sacred, and holy, even though they are done through frauds and violence and not within the marriage state. He was not content simply to utter the above-mentioned affronts everywhere publicly, but he also took care, to the limits of his power, to have them portrayed skilfully and lavishly in words and pictures, the more quickly to allure people into hearing, seeing, and holding fast to these things.[1] But still worse remains: the more subtly to deceive, he mixed honey with poison and sweetness with venom, like poisonous serpents lying under the green grass of devotion. And he does this by drawing together diverse materials, which often are scarcely to his purpose, aside from such deception, so that, by seeming to have experienced and studied many things, he would be the better believed and have greater authority.

---

[1] Gerson was particularly sensitive to the evil influence of lascivious pictures upon youth. Connolly writes: "Against the many influences that might have corrupted the youth of the city, he set up a cry of protest, and demanded of the public authorities that they take means to remove from the shops and public places images that were suggestive of evil." James L. Connolly, *John Gerson, Reformer and Mystic* (Louvain: Uystpruyst, 1928), p. 87.

I request, therefore, Lady Justice, a swift, fitting remedy for all these offenses and others too numerous for this small petition to contain, but which his book furnishes more evidence of than would be necessary.

After Chastity's petition had been clearly and openly read, one could see that the entire Court there and the whole noble company displayed indignation in their faces and by their appearance. Nonetheless, since wise and moderate voices asked that the defendant be heard and because the Foolish Lover was accused but not present — for he had already gone to that low place from which nobody returns — the question was raised whether there were in the Court of Christianity supporters, spokesmen, or anyone favorable to him. [.
Then, behold, there arose innumerable men and a great multitude, young and old, of all sexes and ages, who, without preserving order, strove haphazardly, one to excuse, another to protect, another to praise him. Another sought pardon for him because he was young and foolish when he wrote and had since done full penance. "In my youth," he says, "I made various writings through vanity." Another supported him because he was so distinguished and so very learned, and because in the French tongue he did not have an equal. Still others defended him because he had spoken the truth so eloquently about all estates, not sparing the Noble or the Common, neither country nor nation, neither the Secular nor the Clergy. "And what evil is there," said one defender more skilful than the others, "What evil is there, I pray, if this man of such great perception and learning and fame should have wished to compose a book in which characters are introduced with great skill, each one speaking according to his own law and nature? Did not the prophet say in the person of a fool, 'There is no God'? [2] And wise Solomon, did he not specifically compose the entire Ecclesiastes in such a manner? And, therefore, he is saved and defended from a hundred errors which are written in this book. If this Lover spoke frivolously, it is simply because he wished to portray the characteristics of Venus, or of Cupid, or of a foolish lover. Did not Solomon in his Canticles speak as a lover, using words which could lead men into evil? Nevertheless, people read

---

[2] Ps. XIII.1; and LII.1.

him. If he says in the character of Reason that all things ought to be named by their own names, his motives are obvious. Truly, what evil is there in names, if it is not there intentionally? Names are like other names: therefore, once a thing is understood by one name and then by another, what could it matter which name is used so long as the thing is understood? Certainly there is nothing in Nature shameful. For shame arises only from sin; yet every day words are made using names associated with sin, such as homicide, theft, frauds, pillaging. [3] Finally, if he has spoken of Paradise and of sacred things, why is he slandered for this, for which he should be praised highly? Admittedly, there is some evil in his book, but it contains much more that is good. Let every man receive the good and reject the evil. For he declares expressly that he attacks only evil men and women, and if anyone should feel himself guilty, let him amend his own life. Indeed, there is no man so wise that he does not sometimes err; nay, even the great Homer nodded. Moreover, what ought to incline this Court of Christianity to mercy and to wise goodness is our knowledge that St. Augustine and nearly all other teachers erred in some ways, but they nevertheless are not accused on account of that, nor condemned, but rather honored. And truly he must have a beautiful rose in his garland who blames this rose which is called the Roman de la Rose."

[33]

At these words it was clearly apparent to the friends and supporters of the Foolish Lover that his case was won with no hope of rejoinder. The one smiled upon the other, and, looking at one another and laughing loudly, they exchanged significant glances. The Theological Eloquence, advocate of the Christian Court, arose. He, [4] the beloved of both Conscience and Chastity, at their request as well as in fulfillment of duty, arose with a temperate manner, great authority, and respected gravity. Wise and excellent in learning, he stood for a while with face cast down, the image of a man deep in thought. Then at precisely the right moment with a serene countenance, he looked up. Turning his glance toward Justice and

---

[3] See Cicero, *De officiis,* I.xxv.128.

[4] Although feminine in grammatical gender, Theological Eloquence is clearly masculine according to Gerson's conception, since he uses the personal pronoun *il,* "he," a number of times. Despite this fact, both Pierre Col and Christine de Pisan consistently speak of *Dame Eloquance Theologienne.*

all her companions, he opened his mouth, and with a sonorous voice, pleasant and moderate, he began to defend the case thus:

"If it were pleasing to God, whom you indeed represent, O Lady Justice, I would wish that the author who is here accused could himself come forward in his own person, by returning from death unto life. For then there would be no necessity for further verbosity, nor would the Court need to busy itself with a prolix accusation. For I believe that swiftly, voluntarily, and gladly he would confess his crime and would be ready to seek pardon by making satisfaction for it. Many conjectures predispose me to this [34] judgment, especially what some have mentioned, thinking to excuse him, that in his lifetime he repented and subsequently wrote books of true Faith and holy doctrine. I am here present a witness for him. It is regrettable that youthful folly or some other evil inclination should have seduced such a clerk to apply so irresponsibly his fine mind, vast knowledge, erudition, and talent in rime to such frivolity. Would to God that he had used them better! Alas, good Friend and wise man, alas! Were there not enough foolish lovers in this world, without your having made yourself a part of this crowd? Were there not enough people to lead and teach them in their foolishness, without your having made yourself their captain, leader, and master? He is a fool who does foolish things. Foolishness is not good sense. He who debases himself and takes on himself the task of infamy is inviting severe criticism. In truth, you were worthy of a different command, another office. Vice and sin, believe me, are all too easily learned, nor is there any need for a teacher. Human nature, especially in youth, is far too prone and inclined to falling, plunging, and immersing itself in impurity and the filth of all carnality. There was no need for you to drag them or forcibly push them in. For what thing can more easily be seized and inflamed with the fire of filthy desires than the human heart? Why, therefore, do you fan this stinking fire with the winds of the most frivolous of all words and with the authority of your own person and your own example? If at that time you did not fear God or his vengeance, why did not the punishment imposed upon Ovid make you prudent and cautious? Surely, the honor of your calling should have restrained you. Without a doubt, you would have been ashamed if, in broad daylight, you had been found in the place of foolish, light women who prostitute themselves for money, and even of speaking to them the way you write. Yet you do worse, you exhort to worse things. Because of your foolishness, you have put to death, murdered, and poisoned thousands and thousands of men through various shameful actions, and still yet do so daily by your foolish book. Nor can you be excused in your method of speaking through characters, as in the following I will clearly prove to you. And yet I cannot possibly say all I need to say in a single statement.

O God, Most Excellent, Most Great! If you, Foolish Lover (for thus you wish to be called), if you had repented in your lifetime of the numerous works which you wrote in your youth through vanity, why did you suffer these things to last and to survive? Ought they not to have been burned? Such a setting forth of poisons [35] is evil, either venom at the table or fire among oil and straw: he who will scatter fire everywhere and not take it away, how will he be absolved for the houses which are burned? Is there any worse or more searing fire than the fire of lechery? And what houses are more precious than human souls, as is clearly pointed out in the petition of Lady Chastity? For those souls ought to be the sacred temples of the Holy Spirit, and yet what burns and inflames these spirits more than dissolute, filthy, lecherous words, writings, and pictures? [5] We see that pious, holy, and honorable words, writings, and images incite to devotion, as Pythagoras said. For this reason, sermons are made and images in churches. Much more easily, on the other hand, evil and impure words draw to profligacy; nor is there anyone who does not know this by experience, and many histories show it.

But, O good friend! superfluously and in vain I speak to you, who are absent, for this deed truly displeases you and would displease, as I said before, if you were present. And if at that time you were ignorant of this thing, you have learned in the meantime by means of many heavy scourges, either in the purgatorial fire or through penitence in this world. You will say perhaps that you were unable to recover your book once it had been published, or,

---

[5] It is interesting to note that Gerson is the first critic to refer to the pictures which illuminate the manuscripts. No other participant in the Quarrel does so. Recent scholarship has returned to the subject. See, for example, John V. Fleming, *The Roman de la Rose: A Study in Allegory and Iconography* (Princeton: Princeton University Press, 1969).

perhaps, that it was taken without your knowledge or in some other way, I do not know. I do know, however, what that one whom you have very often recalled, Berengier, the disciple of Peter Abelard, said at the hour of his death. In that hour when truth declares the one who has done well — and it was the day of the Appearance of Our Lord — with his dying breath he said, "My God, today you will appear to me for my salvation, as I hope, on account of my penitence; or for my hard damnation, as I fear, on account of those whom I deceived by perverse doctrine, whom I was not able to lead again to the true way of your Sacrament." [6] Thus perhaps you too will say briefly: it is not a jest, neither is anything more dangerous than to disseminate a perverse doctrine in the hearts of men. For their punishment, especially those who are damned, grows more and more every day, or, if they should be in the purgatorial fire, their liberation is impeded and delayed.

Many teachers wonder whether Solomon, wisest of all men on earth, was saved. Why? Because before his death, he did not take care to demolish the temples of the idols, which he had commanded to be made on account of his foolish love of foreign women. Repentance is not sufficient unless the occasion of sin for oneself [36] and for others is destroyed, as much as lies in one's power. Nevertheless, whether your repentance was accepted by God or not — I hope it was — I speak only of the deed itself and of your book. And because you, wisely, do not defend it, I shall turn all my complaint to those who, against your own better judgment and will and to the grave prejudice of your honor and salvation, strive either distortedly or perversely to sustain, nor to sustain only, but even to add to and to enhance your foolishness. And in this thing they confound you, for, thinking to defend you, they displease and harm you. Although wishing to please you, they are like violent and headstrong surgeons who think to cure but, in fact, kill; they are like a foolish lawyer who thinks he helps his client but rather destroys his case at law. I, on the contrary, will perform this service in memory of your spirit, and I will do this kindness and this service for it, because of your study and learning; I will condemn those things which you wish utterly to be condemned. What sort

---

[6] Berengier of Tours (c. 1010-1088) denied the doctrine of transubstantiation.

of ignorance is this, dear friends? And what foolish presumption have I heard here from all of you? From you, I say, who would excuse from all folly or error the man who condemns himself, who bears the title of his own condemnation on his brow. I repeat, 'condemnation.' Don't look askance at me. By your very words, he conducts himself like a Foolish Lover.

Truly, if I were to say slanderous things about such an author, scarcely could I accuse him more harshly than by naming him the Foolish Lover. This name bears the heavy burden and the weight of excessive lustfulness and bestial carnality, which murders all the virtues and throws fire wherever possible. Thus say Plato, Archyta of Tarentum, [7] Cicero, and many others. Who burned great Troy cruelly with fire and flame? A Foolish Lover. Who caused more than a hundred thousand nobles to be destroyed: Hector, Achilles, Priam, and others? A Foolish Lover. Who banished from the city King Tarquin and all his lineage? A Foolish Lover. Who deceived through fraud and perjury honorable young girls, nuns, and virgins sacred to God? A Foolish Lover. Who forgets God, holy men and women, Paradise, and his own destiny? A Foolish Lover. Who holds as nothing parents, friends, and every virtue? A Foolish Lover. From whence have come forth civil conspiracies, whence rapine and robberies? From supporting foolish prodigality. Whence the bastards, whence the abortions and strangling of infants, whence the hatreds and deaths of husbands? And, in a word, all manner of evil and folly? Because of the Foolish Lover. But I see that, in actuality, you wish to excuse him from his foolishness by using this title, this term of abuse, saying that in a foolish man one ought to seek nothing except foolishness. But, in God's name, good friends, to a fool his own foolishness must be made manifest, and much more so to a wise man when he does a foolish thing, and, more especially, if this thing is a grievous danger to a great kingdom, and the vile destruction of good morals and of Lady Justice and of all her noble Court of Christianity. All of you see plainly, therefore, the many reasons why Lady Chastity complains. Modesty, Fear, and my mistress Lady Reason are afflicted with pain; in short, the whole Court and the group of Noble Virtues (you see it in their bearing) are greatly displeased. And why should

[37]

---

[7] A philosopher of Tarentum, c. 400-365 B.C.

they not be? Because, you will say, the author does not speak here, but others, who are introduced by him. This defense is too slight for so great a crime. I ask you, if someone should declare himself the enemy of the king of France, and, under such a name, he should also make war on the king, should this name prevent him from being a traitor and brought to death? Surely not. If in the person of an heretic or a Saracen, yea truly of the devil himself, someone writes or sows errors against Christianity in any degree, shall he be excused? Once, a certain man attempted to do that, but immediately by one of the chancellors of the Church of Paris in a formal hearing before the episcopal court he was compelled to recant and to correct his error, notwithstanding what he said in the presence of his learned judges. When he said, "I speak as a Jew," the chancellor replied, "You will retract as a Christian." If someone writes notorious books and, by means of introduced characters, defames some person, whether of low or noble or illegitimate birth, the law holds such a writer to be wicked and deserving of punishment. What therefore ought the laws to say, and you Lady Justice, not of a small book, but of a great volume, crammed full of all kinds of disgraceful things, not against men only but also against God and against holy men and women, who love virtue? Tell me, could there not be someone listening who might say to the Prince or to someone from among the great, "Certainly, Lord, I say to you, in the character of a Jealous Man, or of an Old Woman or through a dream, that your wife is very evil and is breaking her marriage vow. Beware, beware, do not put faith in her in anything. And to your daughters, who are still beautiful and young, I counsel them to abandon themselves to the fleshly work, and to any man who will give them a pleasing reward." Tell me, dearest friends, are you so audacious and inex- [38] perienced, that you would judge such a man not to be deserving of punishment, but worthy of support, a favorable hearing, and forgiveness? And more especially if in addition to words, he should send out also books or images and pictures. Further, what is worse: for a Christian clerk to assume the character of a Saracen preaching against the Faith, or for him to introduce a real Saracen speaking or writing against the Faith? Never indeed should the second disgrace be tolerated. Nevertheless, the first, the deed apparently of a Christian, is worse. How much more injurious the secret enemy than the open, from whom a thing is more quickly and easily received, heard, and believed. I will give poison hidden in honey; someone dies; am I excused? I will strike in kissing; I will kill in embracing; will I be free? I will say publicly to some holy person: "Certainly, the enviers and those who hate you say that you are a hypocrite and a cloaked thief and a homicide, and they offer themselves to prove this"; am I to be excused for this slander? Someone dissolute and evil will do and say every kind of lustfulness which he can discover between man and woman in the presence of some innocent girl, saying: "Do not do thus, however much you see us doing such things." Consider well: will he be excused? Certainly not, because Chastity, Fame, the Eye, and Faith do not allow light play or jest; for they are too easily attacked and corrupted.

But I hear clearly what you are muttering together, what one of you previously alleged: namely, that Solomon and David did thus. This is too great an outrage, that some Foolish Lover may be excused by accusing God and his saints, by drawing them into accusation. Nay, this cannot be done. I would wish that this Foolish Lover had not used these characters, except as Holy Scripture did, that is, to reprove evil, in such a way that every man might perceive that condemnation of evil and that approbation of good, and (what is most important) that all those things could have been done without excessive frivolity. But no. Everything seems to be said in his own person; everything seems as true as the Gospel, particularly to those foolish and vicious lovers to whom he speaks. And I regret to say, he incites the more quickly to lechery, even when he seems to reproach it. Truly, the chaste, if they should consider it worthy to give time and trouble to this book of his, to hear it, or to read it, for this reason they would be the worse in the future.   [39]

The teachers tell us that formerly it was not customary for the Canticles of Solomon (however serious they be in themselves) to be read by any save those who were thirty years old or above, lest they find therein any impure carnality. [8] Therefore, what shall

---

8 Cf. Origen's Commentary on the Song of Songs: "For this reason, therefore, I advise and counsel everyone who is not yet rid of the vexations of flesh and blood and has not ceased to feel the passion of his bodily nature,

younger men, faulty and unstable, do with such a book, that is, with such a flame more incendiary than Greek Fire or a glass oven. To the fire, dear men, to the fire. In God's name, withdraw, flee at once, save yourselves, preserve yourselves and your children wisely. There is no better remedy. He who does not flee from the peril will stumble into it and be caught, even as the rat in the lard or the wolf in the wolf trap; like the moth burned by the flame of the candle on account of its light; or the fools and the boys charmed by the beauty of flickering swords or blazing wood, unless someone removes those temptations.

If you should say that there are many good things in this book, are the evil things in it, I ask therefore deleted? Is its fire not more dangerous? Does the hook injure the fish less if it is covered with bait? Does a sword dipped in honey cut less deeply? No! But further, would the pure and good doctrines fail anywhere without mixing in evil? Mohammed, who mixed, with great and deliberate malice, the truths of our Christian faith with his own impure errors, serves as a good example of whether one should preserve and cherish anything good which is mixed with evil. Why did Mohammed do this? In order to attract Christians more readily to his own Law and to cover his own outrages. Does not the devil sometimes say many truths through demoniacs, through enchanters, through magicians, and even through heretics? But this is so, that

---

to refrain completely from reading this little book and the things that will be said about it. For they say that with the Hebrews also care is taken to allow no one even to hold this book in his hands, who has not reached a full and ripe age. And there is another practice too that we have received from them — namely, that all the Scriptures should be delivered to boys by teachers and wise men, while at the same time the four that they call *deuteroseis* — that is to say, the beginning of Genesis, in which the creation of the world is described; the first chapters of Ezechiel, which tell about the cherubim; the end of that same, which contains the building of the Temple; and this book of the Song of Songs — should be reserved for study till the last." Origen, *The Song of Songs: Commentary and Homilies,* trans. R. P. Lawson (London: Longmans, Green and Co., 1957), p. 23. See also St. Jerome, who writes of the education of a young girl that she should start her reading of the Bible with the Psalter, progressing gradually, until finally: "Then at last she may safely read the Song of Songs: if she were to read it at the beginning, she might be harmed by not perceiving that it was the song of a spiritual bridal expressed in fleshly language." *Select Letters of St. Jerome,* trans. F. A. Wright (Cambridge, Mass.: Harvard University Press, 1963), Letter CVII, p. 365.

he may deceive the more covertly: for the evil doctrine in it is the
worse, the more good it contains.

Believe me, not me, but St. Paul the Apostle, [9] Seneca, and
experience, that evil speaking and writings corrupt good morals,
leading to immodest conduct and destroying all sense of shame
— shame which in youth is the especial and principal guardian of
all the good conditions of youth against every evil. A young person
without modesty is lost utterly. Why was Ovid, a learned man
and a most ingenious poet, sent into perpetual exile? He himself
is a witness, that this happened to him on account of his wretched
Art of Loving, [10] which he wrote in the time of the Emperor
Augustus. And he was exiled, despite the fact that he had sent
out another book — *Of the Remedy of Love* — in refutation. Ovid
knew well how to speak through dreams or characters, if he could
have been excused through this.

O God! O holy men and women! O Sacred Court of the Christian Religion! O morals of the present time! A pagan and infidel
judge among pagans condemns a pagan who wrote an instruction
book which incited to foolish love. And yet among Christians and
by Christians such a work, or even worse, is supported, is praised,
is defended! There is no way I can fully express my indignation
and horror at this thing; words fail me in condemning it. It is
clear that there are in this book things even worse than anything
in Ovid. For this Romance contains not only Ovid's *Art of Loving*
but also other books which are there translated, brought together,
and drawn in by force and to no purpose. Meun used both Ovid
and the works of others, which are not any the less dishonorable
or dangerous, like the writings of Heloise and Abelard, and of
Juvenal, as well as other fictions about Mars and Venus, Vulcan
and Pygmalion, Adonis and others — all to serve his perverse end.
Ovid clearly declared that he does not wish to speak of good
matrons or of ladies joined in marriage, nor of those who could
not be loved lawfully. [11] Does the book that you defend do thus?
Nay, rather it mocks all, slanders all, despises all without any

---

[9] I Cor. XV.33: "Be not seduced: Evil communications corrupt good
manners."

[10] See *Tristia*, I.i.

[11] See *Ars amatoria*, I.31-34; II.599-600.

exception, even though it purported to be Christian and spoke
sometimes of celestial things. Why did he not spare glorious and   [41]
holy maidens and innumerable others who preserved chastity in
the temple of their hearts, despite the harshest tortures and cruel
death? Why did he not show that reverence for the holiest of holy
women? [12] But no. He was a Foolish Lover and had no such concern; he chose to spare none, that he might the better persuade
all women to prostitute themselves. And he could not better perform such a task than by making women believe that all are so
inclined, and that they, therefore, could not help doing the same.

Necessity has no law. [13] O what a doctrine! not, indeed, a
doctrine, but blasphemy and heresy. By this rule, he tries to prove
that young men will never be firm or stable in religious life, which
is false doctrine and against experience. But if anyone should wish
to dwell on, reprove, and reproach all the evil things declared in
this book, the day would be shorter than the complaint. Too great
a particularity, in fact, could perhaps do more harm than good to
morality. I could fall into the vice that I reproach. I shall, therefore, cut my words short and speak merely of the article contained
in the petition of Lady Chastity laid forth by Conscience. Now I
feel that I have dealt with the less important Articles, and it is
time for me to proceed to the graver and more inexcusable ones.

The matter is grave, Lady Justice. May your Court be attentive
in giving them a careful hearing, in order to reach a speedy decision.
Certainly, with regard to the said book (if book it deserves to be
called), there is a convenient and apt saying: "The sting lies in
the tail." The mocking laughter of Horace is appropriate here, like
the painter who drew a very beautiful woman, attractive at the
head, but tailing off into a fish. [14] (The harpies were said to be
like this, for they had the faces of virgins but bellies and lower
parts of the most disgusting kind.) Alas, how much impurity is set
down and accumulated in the tail of this book! What blasphemies!
What diabolical wickedness is sown therein! For a while we hear
him talk about paradise, the sweet and chaste Lamb, and the
beautiful little fountain, but then suddenly in his own person he

---

[12] Apparently, a reference to the Holy Virgin.
[13] A medieval commonplace, used, for example, in *Piers Plowman*, XIV.45.
[14] Horace, *Ars poetica*, 2-5.

swiftly recounts his own depraved life! Anyone else would find it
too dishonorable and would blush for shame at doing such a thing.
He encourages all men to make sport of women, virgins or not,
and to do just as he pleases. And — what is the height of evil — he
says that such things are sanctuaries, sacred and estimable acts. He
ought rather to have said execrable and detestable. O what am I
about to say here? Merely to think about these things is surely a
great abomination. My mouth shall not be contaminated further in [42]
speaking, nor your holy ears burdened, nor this Court sullied in
hearing them. I pray you nevertheless, let nothing prejudice my
cause. And if it is true what St. Augustine says, and certainly it
is true, that "To despise the holy word of God is not a lesser evil
than to despise the body of Jesus Christ," the author, in thus
speaking of God and mixing the vilest things with divine and holy
words, committed as much irreverence as if he had thrown the
most precious body of Our Lord Jesus Christ under the feet of
swine or upon a heap of dung. Think what an affront, what ugliness,
and what horror! He could not have done worse by throwing the
text of the gospels or the image of the Crucifix in a deep, disgusting
pit of filth. Aristotle says, as Seneca cites, that "One should never
conduct oneself so reverently and honorably as when one speaks
of God." [15] And speaking of God in this context is to throw out to
the same mud and filth the precious and holy stone of Christian
truth. In this matter, let me say this: He believed that which he
said concerning Paradise, as I believe. Alas, why, therefore, did
he not meditate upon that which he believed? If he did not believe, he was false, heretical, and hypocritical. This is what I conclude from the dissolute life that he glories in and boasts about.

I could argue further, if it would serve any purpose. I could
say how sometimes in the person of Nature, sometimes of Genius,
as Chastity correctly reported, he exhorts and encourages to all
forms of carnality indiscriminately; and he curses all men and
women who do not indulge in it. Nor does he make mention of
marriage, which nevertheless is ordained by Nature. He discourages
restraint in speech, and he promises Paradise to all those who will
behave dissolutely. Anyone who does not believe him, follow his

---

[15] Gerson expresses the same idea at the beginning of his sermon *Videmus
nunc per speculum in enigmate.*

doctrine, and repeat it everywhere is a fool. It is true that this poetic fiction was abstracted from Alanus' great book, *The Complaint of Nature* — but corruptly. Because indeed the greatest part of our Foolish Lover's book is almost completely a translation of the writings of other authors. This I know well: he was humble who deigned to borrow from his neighbors, and he covered himself with the bright-colored plumes of others, as the fables tell us about the little crow. But I am not impressed by such humility. I turn again to Alanus, and I say that he never did speak in such a fashion through a character. For this would have been hardly appropriate, insofar as he execrates and reprobates vices against Nature, and rightly: I do the same thing. Cursed be those who will not desist, and may Justice burn them. But this is not to say that one sin ought to be encouraged so that another sin can be avoided. He would be a foolish physician who would seek to heal one wound or sickness through another, or to extinguish fire with fire. Therefore, whoever desires to excuse this man's intolerable works by saying that it is Nature who speaks, I answer for you, Lady Nature, that you never did counsel sin, nor did you wish anyone to act against the ten commandments, which we call in fact your commandments, the commandments of Nature. He who would say otherwise and contrary — that, according to the Law of Nature, the natural act between man and woman outside marriage is not a sin — would be erring in the Faith. [43]

Lady Justice, I am fully aware that I have been speaking for a long time, but although you and your most learned Court comprehend everything even when it is briefly expressed, I have spoken all too briefly in view of the enormity of this vile crime. You detest all shameful vileness, you who know all the laws and legal codes, and especially those you have heard cited in this particular case, which has been pled without much subtlety. For I know to whom I speak, before whom, and for whom. Therefore, what has been said can be sufficient to condemn and proscribe the said book, just as was done in the case of others which seemed to inflict injury and detriment on our faith and on good morals, just as the Apostles did with regard to the newly converted. [16] Thus the Ancients did likewise with the books of a poet called Archilocus, although they

---

[16] See Acts XIX.19.

were masterly, because they did harm to the good morals of youth more than they brought out the natural goodness of their character. Here, we can see the same offense.

Now, therefore, I should come to an end, except that Lady Reason, wise and good, my Mistress, makes a sign to me that I should speak further. And it is no wonder, for her honor depends greatly upon it. Undoubtedly, she could defend herself; that is evident. But since I have begun and it pleases her to have me continue, I will do so gladly, very briefly, and much more succinctly than the crime itself would require. O all of you who stand forth here on behalf of the Foolish Lover, if this error is irrational which imputes madness to Reason, is it not madness to say that one should speak fully and openly without shame, no matter how dishonorable the words are in the judgment of all men, even of those who were without law and without modesty? If this error, I say, had not been a long time ago heartily condemned by ancient [44] philosophers, this author, or all of you who defend him (nay rather, accuse), would not be so greatly open to condemnation. But the truth is that Cicero, before the Advent of Jesus Christ, in his book *De Officiis,* [17] and other philosophers — and, later, holy teachers whom you may still read — have censured this foolishness; yea, even Good Custom (which is the same as Nature) contemns, despises, and spurns the same. How therefore can it be justified to impose such a character upon Lady Reason — as if those who do not do so were senseless and unreasonable — for the Reason who spoke was not the wise one but the foolish and absurd. In God's name, this character were better projected on swine or dogs than on Reason. Do not oppose my argument in this matter, for some Ancients who claimed to be philosophers were actually called dogs because they held this shameful doctrine. Was not Ham accursed and made a vile slave only because he saw the secret parts of his father Noah and did not cover them? [18] This error was also the error of the Turlupins, [19] who maintained that this was the state of Innocence and the height of perfection on earth. In what man-

---

[17] See I.xxxv.127.

[18] See Gen. IX.21-25.

[19] An heretical sect, condemned in the fourteenth century, which held that nothing natural should be considered shameful.

ner could a more irrational thing be imputed to Reason? In what
manner could greater audacity have been given to all irrational men
than that Reason should speak thus, especially when she utters
enticing things in her conversation which incline men to every kind
of frivolity.

Entrust, entrust your daughters and sons to such a teacher, and,
if they are not wise enough, direct them to the schools of that
Reason! Teach them the way to every evil if they are not able to
find it by themselves. If they do not speak according to the teachings of that Reason, beat them! And, furthermore, by this same
reasoning one could prove that people should go about naked and
do as they please anywhere openly and shamelessly. And I am
convinced that his "Reason" could support that view with her line
of argument. Anyone who believes this should go naked through
the streets, and then he would find out whether Reason would
prevent him from being scorned, booed, and reviled. If at least
Reason had spoken to a learned man knowledgeable about the
nature of things, or to a great theologian who knows that if it had
not been for original sin there would have been no shame, he
would have then had an ample justification. He could then have   [45]
alleged the nudity of Adam and Eve, even though there is a vast
difference between the State of Innocence and ours. For the comparison is as if one were to speak from the healthy to the infirm.
Wine, which would not do harm to the healthy, will render him
unconscious who trembles violently with fevers. Thus it is that in
the present state seeing or hearing carnal acts moves those sinners
who see and hear to the most shameful desires, but within the
State of Innocence it would not have been so. This is clearly apparent, since before sin Adam and Eve were naked and unashamed;
after they sinned, they immediately hid and covered themselves
with great shame. Nor is it difficult to see why one method of
speaking is prohibited more especially than another, even though
the same subject is being discussed. In this particular, there is no
need for me to pause and expound the natural cause; experience
makes that clear enough. It is on account of fantasy which is easily
stimulated, and fantasy is what breeds desire. Thence it is that
Lady Idleness is gate-keeper of foolish love. For when she does
not find the imagination and fantasy of a man busily engaged, she
then, in one way or another, rouses carnal desires in him. There-

fore, there is no better safeguard than keeping oneself busy with some worthwhile task. Hence it happens that a person melancholic, infirm, and of a weak temperament, sometimes will be tempted more burningly by carnality than a person healthy and sanguine, smiling and happy. All this comes forth from fantasy. What wonder if a fire covered with ashes does not burn so quickly as an open fire. The same is true of carnal things said or seen openly. But I return to my argument and say that if the character Reason had spoken to a wise and mature man, it would have perhaps been worthwhile. But no, she speaks to a Foolish Lover. And here the author has observed the rules of my school badly, the rules of rhetoric, which are to consider who is speaking, to whom he speaks, and for what time he speaks. And not only is he at fault in this, but also in many other places where he attributed to a character who speaks inappropriate opinions, as when he introduces Nature speaking of Paradise and the mysteries of our Faith, and Venus swearing by the flesh of God. But even though this is an error in that person whom some people wish to place so far above all other men who ever existed, I don't make much of it. I am far more aggrieved for Lady Reason and Chastity, because of what he chose [46] to be said through wise Reason to the Foolish Lover. He said such follies — shameful, obscene, and impure words, as well as a thorough condemnation of women — which Cupid, who is called the god of Love, had previously forbidden, as if Cupid were more chaste and reasonable than Lady Reason and Chastity. O God! I err; it was not the same author but that one at the beginning whom I speak of. And he built wholly his own work. For the first author had erected, some time earlier, the foundations of the work with his own hands and his own material, and he did not borrow his ideas here and there, nor gather such baseness of stinking filth and excrement as later soiled this work. I do not know whether his successor thought to honor him by his additions, and if he believed that, he was deceived indeed. For to the beginning, which perhaps fitted well enough into his own following deed, he joins, even among Christians, a most shameful conclusion and an irrational middle in opposition to Reason. This end and middle, truly, the pagans in their Republic (as I said earlier), Augustus and the philosophers, never would have allowed or tolerated. And, although the two cases are not alike, holy teachers have also corrected and amended their works.

I conclude therefore before you, Lady Canonical Justice, and before your Court, that a Proviso ought to be put out by unanimous edict against this offense. I conclude nothing against the person of the author: for this belongs to God. But I speak of the error, which is so very great, the extreme gravity of which has been shown previously. And I briefly repeat them here item by item: its extreme error in occasion for sin; in blasphemies; in poisonous doctrines; in the destruction and desolation of poor Christian souls; in the illicit waste of time, which is so precious; resulting in harm to Chastity; in the dissipation of faithfulness of both married and single; in the expulsion of fear and of modesty; in the defamation of Reason; in the great dishonoring of you, Lady Canonical Justice, of your laws and rights, and of all this religious Court of Christianity; nay even truly of all of you, even of the evil men, who from this thing may be made even worse.

[47]

May such a book therefore be put aside and exterminated without any use in the future, especially in those parts in which he employs disreputable and prohibited characters, such as the accursed Old Woman, who ought to be judged to the punishment of the pillory; and Venus, that is, Lechery, which is mortal sin; and the Foolish Lover, who ought not to be allowed to perform foolishness for his own pleasure. There could be no greater perversity nor no way of making him more odious than permitting these things to him. This petition, therefore, pleasing to my God and to you, Lady Justice, accepted by your whole Court, and most useful and lovable to all foolish lovers (however so loudly they may cry out against it), and after they are healed, most peaceful and delectable to them. Yet may no one judge or complain that I accuse anything but the vices and not the people themselves. I make in the name of Chastity and Conscience such a petition and conclusion against all pictures or writings or sayings which move one to lustfulness. For our fragility of itself is too greatly inclined to sin, without outside inflaming and prostration in the depths of vices, far off from the virtues and from God, who is our glory, our love, our salvation, joy, and happiness."

As Eloquence ended this oration, I heard the hour strike, at which my heart flew back again to its first state. And, hearing nothing of the judgment,[20] I was again in my library at Vespers. In the year of grace 1402, May 18. There I took up another matter in order to occupy my heart so that it might not be so likely to take flight. And the material was concerned with the blessed Trinity in divine Unity and Simplicity. Next with the holy Sacrament of the Altar, etc.

[48]

---

[20] Gerson leaves the outcome undecided, a common enough feature of the conventional medieval *disputatio*.

XIII

PIERRE COL'S REPLY TO CHRISTINE DE PISAN

[Pierre Col's letter is addressed only to Christine de Pisan, but it is clearly in reply also to Gerson's treatise. Col repeatedly refers to and criticizes Lady Theological Eloquence, though Christine seems to be his particular bête noire. *Although Col knows full well who wrote the* Traité contre le Roman de la Rose — *as he makes clear in his letter — he never calls Gerson by name. Potansky places this letter between the beginning of June and the beginning of September, 1402. The text is in Ward, pp 56-76.]*

After I had heard people speak of your high understanding, your clear intellect, and of your melodious eloquence, I desired very greatly to see your letters and other small things of like kind. Thus after great care in seeking them, there has come into my hand a certain letter of yours, addressed, as I note, to my Seigneur and especial master, Monsieur le Provost of Lisle, which began: "Reverence, honor," etc. In this letter you make an effort to reproach the very devout Catholic and very excellent theologian, the most divine orator and poet and most perfect philosopher, Master Jean de Meun, in some particular parts of his book of the *Rose.* Yet I myself scarcely dare to open my mouth in praise of this book, lest I should set my foot into an abyss. For as we read of Herod, he did more good to the Innocents through hatred by having them killed than he could possibly have done through love. Perhaps it will be the same for you and others who strive with you to impugn this most noble writer Master Jean de Meun. You will perhaps praise him more in thinking to condemn him than I would be able to praise him if all my members were changed into tongues and employed at the task. For I am unequal to the task not only on account of the dullness of my intellect, the heaviness of my understanding, my weak memory, and my poorly ordered language, but more especially on account of the vast abundance of good things which are in that work impossible to express. It is to these very things that you have called attention in thinking to blame him. Therefore, confident in the truth of the ideas of Jean de Meun himself, I will strive to oppose your argument, which is, I must say, more refined in language than your language is refined by reason, a quality more evident in you than in any of his other adversaries, so far as I know or remember. May my coming forth to defend him not be considered presumptuous or arrogant, for in truth I would never be guilty of such. Rather, I simply desire to be, at least, the least among the disciples of the aforesaid Meun. And since your argument against him is so weak that there is no need of a greater, I do not speak for the most advanced disciples of the aforesaid Meun, but rather for the middle or for those near the bottom, where your argument belongs. I am confident also of the complete rightness [56] of the cause I wish to defend; indeed it could stand on its own merits. Thus the work itself is my shield. Pardon me if I address you familiarly with "tu," for I do it in order to show that this response of mine is well-intentioned: that is to say, it seeks to draw you back to the right path. Besides, the familiar form is exactly what our ancient masters used.

First of all, you begin, without reason, with the chapter in which Reason appears, and you say that she names the secret members of man by their proper names. And I respond to such an argument that God made the things; hence, they are good, and indeed can be called by their proper names. You do say, in fact: "I confess that God created all things pure and clean coming from Himself, so that in the State of Innocence there would have been no wickedness in naming them; but man became impure by the pollution of sin." [1] Further, you use as an example Lucifer, who was first beautiful and whose name was beautiful, but who subsequently

---

[1] Col sometimes quotes Christine word for word; at other times he paraphrases her very closely. For this quotation, see page 48.

was reduced to a horrible ugliness by sin, whereby the name, although it is beautiful of itself, horrifies those who hear it. Besides, you say that the name does not make the thing dishonorable; but the thing, the name. Here you resemble the pelican: you kill yourself with your beak.[2] If you believe that the thing makes the name dishonorable, what name can you give to the thing which would not be dishonorable, if the thing is not changed when the name is. Then I come to the place where you say that in the State of Innocence it was permitted to name the secret members, and that God formed them in such a state. I ask you whether you would speak of the secret members of a two- or three-year-old child — for you would not deny that God creates us all. Would you dare name them by their proper name? If you say no, nevertheless he is in the state of innocence without pollution in word or deed. And it is useless for you to reply that you spoke of original sin, for it came about through disobedience. And if the pollution of our first parents made the secret members so shameful that one is not permitted to name them, I say that by a stronger reason one ought not to call our first parents by name. For they are the ones who sinned; not their members. If you say yes, it is permissible for one to name the secret members of a child, I ask you to tell us to what age it is permitted to name them, and also whether one can name by their name the secret members of an aged man who has been chaste and virginal all his life. Similarly, would you dare to name the secret members of dumb beasts, for they do not sin at all. Thus, can you   [57] teach Reason and the disciples of the aforesaid Meun how they should speak! In fact, in this chapter of Reason, the Lover himself offers a broader and more forceful argument against naming the secret members than you do. And Reason responds to his argument, and yet you do not address yourself to this response at all, as you should have done before you criticized her. Thus there is no more need to answer you with regard to this matter.

But I have seen a work made in the manner of a Complaint in the Holy Court of Christianity, in which Canonical Justice was established as judge, and the virtues around her as her council, the chief and chancellor of which was Wise Understanding, accom-

---

[2] Cf. Eustache Deschamps, Ballade 856, line 21: "Vous vous tuez, com fait li pellicant."

panied by Lady Reason, Prudence, Knowledge, and others as secretaries. Theological Eloquence was advocate of the Court. The promoter of the suits was Conscience, who brought up and presented a request by Chastity, as follows: "To Justice the law giver, who holds the place of God on earth, and to the universal Court of his devout and most Christian religion, Chastity, your faithful subject, humbly supplicates and requests that you provide a remedy and a brief warning against the intolerable deeds which a certain Foolish Lover has been doing and continues to do to me," and he places thereafter eight or nine articles. Now, in truth, I believe I know the one who composed this Complaint, and doubtless he speaks as a clergyman, begging his pardon, about the Foolish Lover. By my faith, I fully share the belief which he expressed when, preaching solemnly on the Day of the Trinity, he said that we can see and know the Trinity only in part and in a mirror darkly. This is the way that he sees, understands, and speaks of a foolish lover, for I think that he never was one, or had even thought of such matters, so much so that I dare say he could render better account of the Trinity, which he has thought about more, than he does of the Foolish Lover. And therefore I would have reason enough to say to all this Complaint that it is not necessary to respond at all, for the whole Complaint is founded on a Foolish Lover, and the author does not know what a foolish lover is. And it is useless to say that, although he is no foolish lover, yet he understands intuitively better than someone who is, or has been one. This may be, but I dare say that one who has been, but no longer is, a foolish lover can understand that state far better than he does. For personal experience has far greater power than what one is told. Truth and right so clearly support the one he calls the Foolish Lover that it will cause me no difficulty to answer the charges that Lady Theological Eloquence brings against him. For by my faith, this good lady has never thought deeply about the matter, as I shall show hereafter. Moreover, I believe that the said Meun was at one time a foolish lover.

[58]

First, then, Lady Theological Eloquence says that Master Jean de Meun carries on his forehead the inscribed title of his condemnation by this word *Foolish Lover,* and she continues: "Who brought great Troy to ruin in former days by fire and flame? A foolish lover. Who caused more than a hundred thousand noble men to be destroyed: Hector, Achilles, and others? A foolish lover. Who exiled King Tarquin from Rome? A foolish lover," — and other such examples. I ask Lady Eloquence if this argument seeks to blame a man for being a foolish lover or to blame the book of the *Rose* because it was made by a foolish lover? If it blames a foolish lover, I will not answer at all. For I admit that being a foolish lover is foolish and irrational, but there is no need for anyone to try to blame a foolish lover more than the book of the *Rose* does. Look well, you who read it; does he not say of the God of Love:

This is the God who leads all astray   [4342] [3]

And afterward:

But let them guard themselves from foolish love,
which so cruelly enflames and burns the heart.   [4593-4]

It is this which has shriveled your skin.   [4606]

His heart entangled in the love of a woman,
For which many men have lost both body and soul.   [13933-4]

It is Love who kindles and fans the glowing embers
Which he has put in your heart.   [6399-400]

Whoever lives rationally
Will never love passionately.   [6884-5]

That those who most indulge in love
Regret most in the end.   [10125-6]

And more than a hundred other places that I will not mention for brevity's sake. But no, one more verse will suffice for all:

Many lose therein, I dare say,
Sense, time, property, body, soul, reputation.   [4627-8]

---

[3] This and all succeeding numbers incorporated into the text which refer to Col's quotation from the *Roman de la Rose* are based upon the edition by Ernest Langlois. The line numbers in Ward's text refer to the edition by Michel, and are therefore difficult to locate in modern editions.

Now, may those who seek to blame the Foolish Lover more than   [59]
Master Jean de Meun does note especially this "reputation," and
I believe they will find nothing to question. And when Master Jean
de Meun calls the secret members of women "Sanctuaries" and
"relics," [4] he does so in order to show the great folly that is in
the Foolish Lover. For a foolish lover thinks only of this little
rosebud, and it is his god and he honors it as his god. Also at this
point he feigns poetically, and to poets and painters there has
always been such license, as Horace says. [5] He, in fact, chooses his
words very well when he calls a woman's secret members sanctuaries, for the gates and walls of a city are by law called holy
because if one uses force or trespasses without leave against them,
he must suffer the consequences. Thus is it with the secret members of a woman; he who uses force there or who without force
unduly trespasses upon them must pay for it. Moreover, the Bible
says that it was customary to sanctify the secret members of the
woman. [6]

But if the argument seeks to blame the book of the Rose because he who made it was a foolish lover, I marvel why Lady
Eloquence does not first draw such conclusions against Solomon,
David, and other foolish lovers, who were long before Meun, whose
books are made a part of holy Scripture and their words a part of
the holy mystery of the Mass. Who caused Uriah the good knight
to be killed by treachery in order to commit adultery with his wife?
A foolish lover. Who caused the temples with the idols to be built
for the love of strange women? A foolish lover — and so many
others that I pass over. [7]

Against these Lady Eloquence ought to speak first, if she wishes
to press her argument. But she does not do so. Do we not read
that St. Peter and St. Paul were firmer in the faith after they had
sinned, and many others similarly? I say that Master Jean de Meun,
because he had been a foolish lover, was very firm in reason; for
the better he knew the folly which is in foolish love by experi-

---

[4] See lines 20807; 21235; 21583-602.

[5] Horace, *Ars poetica,* 9-10.

[6] Ward cites Leviticus XV, but see Gerson, who remarked, "I do not
know what kind of Bible taught you, unless perhaps you had one in your
possession different from ours." See page 147.

[7] Col is here, of course, echoing Gerson's words with conscious irony.

ence, the better was he able to scorn it and to praise reason. And
when he made this book of the *Rose,* he was no longer a foolish
lover (and had repented of being one), as is clear from his speaking
so well of Reason. If he had not known, loved, and understood
Reason, he could not have spoken as he did. And it is always true
that a foolish lover does not know, love, or understand Reason.
And thus he says, in the chapter of Nature when he speaks of   [60]
Paradise, that the things of the Garden of Delight are only foolishness. And concerning the fountain of Narcissus he says:

> God! what a good and pleasing fountain,
> Where the healthy become sick.   [20421-2]

And that it

> Brings death to the living.   [20625]

How could he show better that he was not a foolish lover and that
he loved Reason than by blaming the Garden of Delight and the
things that are in it; and by praising Reason and by putting another
part in the Garden, in which he depicts so nobly the Trinity and
the Incarnation by the Carbuncle and by the olive tree which takes
its growth from the dew of the fountain, etc.[8] As soon as he began
his part of the book, he took up Reason immediately and God
knows it meant a lot to him; he had difficulty in stopping. So
much so that he was hardly faithful to the first author's intent.
And do not think that what he says in his *Testament* — "I have
made in my youth many works through vanity" — refers to the
book of the *Rose.* For truly as I will prove, he meant various ballades, rondeaux, and virelais that we do not have in writing, at least
I don't. But let us come to your point. Lady Eloquence, addressing
her words to those who support this Foolish Lover, says thus: "Is
this not," says she, "madness to say that one ought to speak bluntly
and crudely and without shame, however dishonorable the words
in the judgment of all people," etc? Ha! Lady Eloquence, you are
constrained here to present your original premise badly, on which
you found all your subsequent argument. But do not hold a grudge
against the man who causes you to do so, for I really believe that

---

[8] Lines 20509-78.

he does not do this knowingly. Certainly, he found little to please him in this most noble book of the *Rose,* because he scarcely read it, or, as I prefer to believe, he was displeased precisely because he had read it little.[9] Yet since his intellect surpasses that of so many others, I am convinced that, if he had read the work and reread it thoughtfully several times, he would have been compelled to praise, value, love, and honor it. See here, see here, the words of Reason:

> Sweet friend, without bringing ill-repute on myself,
> I can indeed name openly and by its proper name [61]
> A thing which is nothing if not good.
> In truth, I can speak of evil explicitly without
> Being harmed. [6945-50]

He does not say that one has to speak of them. He says that one can so speak: this is not at all a duty or a license. I admit that it would be an evil to seek out opportunities to speak of the work of nature and to be cunningly ingenious at speaking of it for mere pleasure — therein lies the impurity that some men abominate so greatly. This is the point made by Cicero in *De Officiis*[10] and other philosophers who spoke similarly of such matters. But when one speaks on many, different subjects and, without any special predilection, mentions the secret members, it is quite proper for him to do so. This is what Jean de Meun does in the chapter of Reason. And, by God, it is fitting to speak of them at least once, if one does not overstress their importance; and their importance is not overstressed since he speaks of them by name once and never again. And so it is permissible to speak in the way that Reason speaks of them. Thus Holy Scripture names them by their proper name and quite rightly. So do law books in many places. And besides the secret members are necessary and useful, and profitable, and beautiful, and good. Further, the Bible forbids a man who has had them cut off to enter a church.[11] And they are named there very properly, and I do not believe that Jesus Christ himself had a member that one could not honorably name. You, as well as your com-

---

[9] Ward's text reads *noyant* for the MS. reading *voyant.*
[10] I.xxv.127-8.
[11] Ward incorrectly cites Leviticus XXI, but see Deuteronomy XXIII.1.

panions, call people by their surnames, which were invented in
order to be the more specific, since the proper names are common
to many. Reason does not speak of the work wherein pollution
lies, but simply names the members belonging to this act. And,
other matters laid aside, if the names are displeasing to some people, they are not displeasing to all. I say this on account of what
Lady Eloquence says: "The words are so very dishonorable in the
judgment of all people." There is surely no case for saying that
good custom forbids speaking plainly. Whether the custom is good
or bad, I won't speak to that. But to say that women are not accustomed to speak so plainly, Lady Eloquence will scarcely win
the day. For in the chapter on Reason, we read:

> If women do not name them in France,
> It is only because it is not customary there.   [7131-2]

And he says "in France," of course, because his book is in French;   [62]
thus it may well be that in places other than France women name
them openly. Yet I am amazed at the custom. For women certainly
call their own private parts by their proper names. They choose
not to name a man's. But I do not see that their parts are more
honorable than man's.

See further what Lady Eloquence says: "he observes badly the
rules of rhetoric, for he ought to have noted to whom Reason
spoke. If she had spoken to a layman, a clerk, or a theologian, it
would have been one thing. But she spoke to a Foolish Lover, who
by such words can be incited to carnality, as a great clerk or theologian would not be." And it seems by her words that being a
clerk, a philosopher, or a theologian is not compatible with being
a foolish lover, that they are irreconcilable. Alas, it is, it has been,
and it will forever be far otherwise. Look at the examples of David,
Solomon, and others. Some teachers even say that Solomon made
the Canticles on account of his love of Pharaoh's daughter; [12] yet
he was held the wisest man of his time or before. In short, one
could bring forth more than a thousand examples of people who

---

[12] This view was held by Theodore of Mopsuesstia, who believed that
the Song of Songs was Solomon's reply to the opponents of his marriage to the
Egyptian princess. See Origen, *Song of Songs, Commentary and Homilies,*
trans. R. P. Lawson (London: Longmans Green & Co., 1957), p. 7.

were clerks and at the same time foolish lovers. For they are as compatible with one another as being at once clerk and knight, as were Pompey, Julius Caesar, Scipio, Cicero, and others. But I believe well that because the one who has made this complaint is a clerk, philosopher, and theologian without being a foolish lover, he thinks that all others are like him. And is it not possible that even he in the future may be a foolish lover? By God, it is so; and he would not be any the less a clerk therefore, at least at the beginning of the foolish love. Also, for God's sake, naming the secret members twice or thrice does not move a man to foolish loving, when it is necessary to name them. When Reason names them, she exhorts the Foolish Lover to desist from foolish love. And in speaking of numerous things, she comes properly to speak of the secret members. Truly, if he had always been thus occupied, Lady Idleness would never have opened the gate of the garden to him. Yet although he already was a Foolish Lover, Reason moved him somewhat toward desisting from it, for which the God of Love reproached him. It is clear that in the chapter of Reason Master Jean de Meun did not stoop to speak of the secret members merely on account of his fondness for speaking bluntly and bawdily but because it suited his purpose in showing the foolishness of those who claim that it is never permissible to name them by their proper names under any circumstances. This is made clear in other [63] places where he speaks of the work of nature but does not name it by its own name, as in the chapter of the Friend and of the Old Woman, where he speaks of the "play of love," the "task of love," and "this dance." [13] Thus it is inaccurate to say that he follows the rules of rhetoric poorly, for he shows clearly that he knew them by nature and by study. I dare say that anyone who reads and understands him will realize that Master Jean de Meun could hardly have spoken in any other way. And when Lady Eloquence says that he has Nature speak of God, I say that she can and ought to do it and that the handmaiden can well speak to her master. Similarly, in the *Soliloquies,* St. Augustine has the devout soul ask the earth and other elements whether they are his God. They answer no and tell the soul to seek higher. [14] Augustine says afterward

---

[13] See lines 834; 9829; 9851; 14319.
[14] PL, 40, col. 888-9. Cf. *Confessions,* X.vi.

that the responses of natural things are the testimony of God. Also Meun wishes to show that it is natural and Christian to speak of Nature, and since he was a poet, as I have said, it pleased him to speak of everything by a fiction. Further, Lady Eloquence says: "This Foolish Lover makes Reason say what Cupid had earlier forbidden and had made then a manner of reproaching." "O! heavens! " says she, "this was not the same author, but the one on whose beginning this Meun built up his own work: the foundations were good and natural, and this Meun built a heap of filth on it."

Certainly, this was well said! To what purpose, I ask her, does Cupid give away a little rose-bud, that is, bring about the downfall of a foolish lady-love. And is it not a great contradiction to say that he blames Reason, who chastises the Lover for being a Foolish Lover, and praises Cupid, who teaches how one can excel in the art? But you, Christine de Pisan, cannot be silent on this matter: thus you respond to Reason's remark that "In the amorous war, it is better to deceive than to be deceived," by arguing that "It follows that both are good, which cannot be, in my judgment." If you had refrained from writing this argument, it would have been to your credit. It is not a subject for serious writing; no, it is a proposition for school children set apart from their fellows to argue. And did Jesus Christ not say that it would have been better for Judas never to have been born than to have betrayed his master? It would follow therefore, according to your argument, that both of these are good. One must not take words literally in this way, but rather according to what was previously said and the intention [64] of the author. The crucial verse preceding the four that you have quoted reads:

But these are the least deceived.   [4398]

I do not believe that this says that it is good to deceive. Furthermore, I say it would not be better, that is, that it would harm me less to pretend to love you in order to enjoy your body than it would if, for this same purpose, I were truly a foolish lover, for in that state I should lose "my learning, my sense, my time, castle, body, soul, reputation," as he said. For all the evils which take place in the first case take place in the second, but all those which take place in the second do not necessarily do so in the first. Nevertheless, I hold that these four verses, beginning, "For it is better, dear Master," [4399] and certain others have been interpolated. And this fact irritates me greatly. For I do not see what can be added or withdrawn without harming the text.

But let us go further. You and Lady Eloquence have exclaimed over the dishonorableness to be found in this chapter of the Old Woman, where, you both say, one finds nothing but filth, and similarly in the chapter of Jealousy; and you say that you would really like to find someone capable of justifying it for you. "What end is served by the many dishonorable words which this book contains?" "But," you say, "I do not condemn the author in all places in the aforementioned book," as if you wish to say that you condemn him in this particular place, and therefore set yourself up as a judge although you have spoken out of prejudice and outrageous presumption. Oh excessively foolish pride! Oh opinion uttered too quickly and thoughtlessly by the mouth of a woman! A woman who condemns a man of high understanding and dedicated study, a man who, by great labor and deliberation, has made the very noble book of the *Rose,* which surpasses all others that ever were written in French. When you have read this book a hundred times, provided you have understood the greater part of it, you will discover that you could never have put your time and intellect to better use. Indeed, he who wrote the Complaint of Lady Eloquence was more delicate and gracious than you. For he says at the end of the Complaint that he did not hear the sentence given. However, as Terence says, "Truth engenders hatred; flattery, friends"; [15] and I suspect it is because Meun spoke the truth that you wish to bite him. But I advise you to keep your teeth to [65] yourself. I answer Lady Eloquence and you by the same means, and I say that Master Jean de Meun in his book introduced characters, and made each character speak according to his nature, that is, the Jealous Man as a jealous man, the Old Woman as an old woman, and similarly with the others. And it is wrong-headed to say that the author believes women to be as evil as the Jealous Man, in accordance with his character, declares. This is clearly not

---

15 *Andria,* 68; "obsequium amicos, veritas odium parit."

true of the author. He merely recites what any jealous man says
about women invariably, and Meun does this in order to demonstrate and correct the enormous irrationality and disordered passion
of jealous men. A jealous man is moved to say so much evil of
women in general, and not just of his own, because, I believe,
normally a married man, before he becomes jealous, thinks that
he has the best wife in the world, or at least as good as any alive.
His belief comes, it seems to me, from two sources: the love he
has for her and the fact that a wife conducts herself with as much
grace and dignity as she can in the presence of her husband. After
all, one does not easily mistrust what one loves. This love arises
because the woman belongs to him and one's own possessions
always seem finer than another's. Let us suppose that in his absence
she behaves bawdily. In such a case, as St. Jerome says in one of
his letters, a man is the last to know the evils in his own home. [16]
I believe there are plenty of other reasons too. But in any case,
whatever his reason, experience shows what I have previously said,
that is, that a man before he becomes jealous believes his wife to
be the best or as good as any other, particularly in the matter of
chastity. It is wise for a married man to think in this way, as
Terence wisely says, that is to say, moderately; [17] otherwise, there
could be no peace among married people. This was the way in
which Aspasia brought accord between Xenophon and his wife, as
Cicero recounts in his rhetoric. [18] Thus, when jealousy strikes a
husband, leading him to suspect the one he had previously considered so good that he saw no evil or guilt in her, then suddenly,
as so often happens, that rage and unbridled passion, Jealousy,
which is rightly called the treacherous evil, drives him to say that
all women are like her. And this is what Aristotle says in his
Rhetoric: that the man who has an evil neighbor believes that all   [66]
neighbors are like him. [19] A knight is famous as the strongest, the
most adept, the most skillful in arms, and the most courageous in
a realm; and everyone holds him to be such. Then a strange knight
comes and vanquishes him in combat. Everybody would then believe that this stranger would be able to vanquish every other

---

[16] PL, 22, col. 1203: "Solemus mala domus nostrae scire novissimi."
[17] *Andria,* 60-61: "ut nequid nimis."
[18] *De Inventione,* I.xxxi.51-55.
[19] *Rhetoric,* II, ch. 21.

knight in the kingdom. In like manner, does a jealous man regard all women, when he believes his own to have been "vanquished" — especially those men who were convinced that their wives were good and chaste, until Jealousy struck. Now to the examples of Lady Eloquence. "If a man declares himself the enemy of the king of France," Lady Eloquence says, "and under this name makes war on him; if in the character of a Saracen a man sows errors in the Faith, will he be excused for it?" And other similar examples, which are scarcely to the point. I ask her, however, if Sallust recites the conspiracy of Catiline against the Republic of Rome, is he guilty for this? Further, if Aristotle recites the opinions of the ancient philosophers containing errors in philosophy, is he the disseminator of errors by doing this? Moreover, if Holy Scripture recites the abominable sins of Sodom and Gomorrah, does it exhort one to commit such sins? When you go to a sermon, do you not hear the preachers castigate the vices that men and women commit every day, so that they might lead them into the right way? In good faith, damoiselle, it is true. One ought to call to mind the foot on which one limps in order to walk better. Ha! Lady Chastity, is this the praise you wish to give to Master Jean de Meun, who has valued you and all other virtues so highly and blamed all vices that the human understanding can conceive? Yes, as the human understanding can conceive: do not smirk about it. I say that he who reads his book well, and often, in order the better to understand it, will find there exhortation to flee all vices and to pursue all virtues. And does he not say in the chapter of the Jealous Man that:

> No one who lives chastely
> can come to damnation?   [9011-2]

And in the chapter of Reason:

> He who goes seeking pleasure,
> Do you know what happens to him?
> He becomes a foolish wretch and serf   [67]
> of the Prince of all the vices.
> This pleasure-seeking is the root of all evils,
> as Cicero says.   [4425-30]
> ... ...

Youth drives men to folly,
frivolity, ribaldry, lechery,
and all manner of excess.   [4463-5]

And in order the better to blame vice he speaks as if vice lay
outside man, just as, in the chapter of the Jealous Man, he says
that all the vices made poverty leap out of hell and come to earth
[9527-40]. And of Shame he says that she restrains and controls
[14107-8]. Yet he speaks more against men than against women.
Does he not condemn, in the chapter on Nature, twenty-six vices
with which men [20] are corrupted? [19225-37]. And in innumerable
other places which I pass over. In the chapter on Nature he says
that clerks abandoned to vice ought to be punished more than lay
men and ordinary people [18663-6], and that gentility resides in
virtue. Among these virtues, he includes honoring ladies and dam-
oiselles [18689-96]. In God's name, this is no attack on the whole
feminine sex. I say this in response to your accusation in the closing
words of your letter. St. Ambrose, in one of his sermons, blames
the feminine sex more, for he says that it is a sex accustomed to
deceiving. In truth, you do also — you blame them more than Meun
when you say that if one read the book of the *Rose* before queens,
princesses, and other great ladies, they would have to blush with
shame. Why should they blush? It appears that they would feel
themselves guilty of the vices that the Jealous Man recites of
women.

Neither does he condemn religion, as Lady Eloquence says. It
is very true that he says that hypocrisy

Betrays many a region by semblance of religion.   [10473-4]

He does not say by religion, but by the *semblance* of religion. For
as he says:

Who would clothe Isengrim in the fleece
of Dame Belin, instead of a sable mantle.   [11123-5]

---

[20] Col is here guilty of the same kind of manipulation of terms as in his
deliberate conflation of state of innocence with State of Innocence. Here, he
plays with *man*, "humanity," vs. *man*, "male."

And this is what Lady Eloquence and you have said in other words,   [68]
that is, of mingling honey with poison in order the more to injure.
And when Lady Eloquence reports that he says that young men
are not at all stable in their faith, I say that when a young man
enters a religious order because of youth rather than devotion, that
he is not firm in it. And this is what Master Jean de Meun says in
the chapter of the Old Woman; and here are his own words:

> So I say to you that
> When a man enters a religious order
> And later regrets it, he is almost
> ready to hang himself in his dismay.   [13967-70]

And thus it is clear that he speaks there of a man who repents of
having entered into a religious order, as they often have. Then he
says afterward:

> He will never know how to make
> Shoes or hood or
> Cowl large enough to hide what
> Nature has put in his heart.   [14009-12]

And a little after he says:

> By my soul, fair son, thus it is
> With every man and woman
> As far as natural appetite goes.   [14087-9]

It is certainly not in accord with man's natural appetite to vow
to abstain from meat and to be chaste and poor all his life, or
even to promise to be faithful to one woman, or, on the other
hand, a woman, to one man. As Lady Eloquence herself suggests,
our frailty is inclined to vice. Does she mean to praise the vices
by this? Not at all. So, if Master Jean de Meun says that natural
appetite is not inclined to religion but to the contrary, he does
not wish by this to blame religion and praise its contrary. But you
will say to me that I recite the good words and not the evil, which
incite to lubricity and teach Jealousy how to take the castle. And
Lady Eloquence says that he wishes to drive all women out of
Chastity. I answer and say to you that in all manners of war it
is a greater advantage to be the defender than the assailant, if

one is warned ahead of time. For example, suppose Jealousy has   [69]
had a strong castle [21] constructed and has placed in it good sentries
to guard it, but the castle is nevertheless captured by a certain
kind of assault. If Jean de Meun has described the way in which
it was captured, has he not given a great advantage to the castle
guards by showing them how it was captured, so that they may in
the future block the gap or place better guards there and thus
lessen the chances of the assailants. By God, it is true! Let us
take for granted that it is an advantage, as I noted above, to be a
defender, and also that Meun described the procedure for capture
in the common language of men and women, young and old, that
is, in French. When Ovid wrote the *Art of Love,* he wrote in
Latin, which women did not understand. Therefore, he gave it only
to the assailants to teach them how to capture the castle. This was
the aim of his book, without speaking through characters. But he,
as Ovid, gave all his teaching. On account of this, he was exiled,
because of the very great jealousy of the Roman husbands. In fact,
this motive was the beginning, middle, and end of the reason for
his exile, such was the enormously cruel jealousy of the Roman
husbands. [22] As I have heard those who have been to Italy say, the
wife of the least jealous husband of that country and of Rome is
more strictly watched than the wife of the most jealous one in
France. And, therefore, if Ovid was exiled because of jealousy, it
was as if he were a man writing against the faith. If he recants, he
will not be exiled at all, but his book will be burnt. And the book
for which Ovid was exiled remains, will remain, and has remained
in all Christendom. And Ovid also recanted by making the book
of the *Remedy of Love.* Truly, I do not understand at all how this
exile can be justified by Reason. I say that if a book is cause of
its author's exile, the book itself ought to be exiled first. But
apropos of what Lady Theological Eloquence says, that a wine
which will not injure a healthy man will drive a man who trembles
from fever out of his senses, I say that whereas a glance by the

---

[21] Col's word is *chastel* and throughout this section he is puckishly playing
with the words *chaste,* "chaste," *chasteté,* "chastity," and *chastel,* "castle."

[22] Ward indicates an ellipsis at this point. There is nothing to justify it
in the MS.

sister [23] or wife of a Roman or Italian will give occasion to the
husband, as I have heard say, of poisoning or murdering her, in
France even a kiss would be no cause for a wife to be scolded or
slapped. There is no point in saying that Jean de Meun, in com-
posing his book, drew on Ovid's *Art of Love* and books by many
others, for the more varied the forms of attack that he describes
the better he teaches the defenders to guard the castle: and it was
for this purpose that he wrote it. In fact, an acquaintance of mine,
in his efforts to free himself from foolish love, borrowed the
Roman de la Rose from me, and I have heard him swear by his
faith that it was this book which helped him most to disentangle
himself. I say this because you ask: "How many have become
hermits or entered into religion?" and "Who took great trouble
for nothing." Further, the Old Woman whom you and Lady Eloquence have blamed so much, said in protest, before she preached
to Fair Welcome:

[70]

> I will gladly tell you ahead of time,
> That I do not wish to lead you into love,
> But if you wish to dabble in it,
> I will gladly point out for you
> Both the ways and paths
> Through which I had to travel . . . [12970-5]

And afterwards she says explicitly to Fair Welcome that she
preaches to him so that he will not be deceived:

> Any man who believes a lover's oaths
> Is surely a fool. [13139-40]

If his book contains very bawdy words which degrade the feminine
sex, it is simply because he quotes other authors who use them,
for, as he says, he does nothing more than quote. Thus, it seems
to me that one ought to blame the authors rather than those who
quote them, as I said before. But you will say to me: "Why does
he quote them?" I say that he did it in order to teach more effectively how gatekeepers should guard the castle. Besides, these
words are appropriate there. For his purpose was to continue the

---

[23] The text reads "*fourme*," which seems to be the reading of the MS.
Ward suggests "*cousine*" as a reading. We prefer "*sœur*."

subject initiated by Guillaume de Lorris, and in so doing to speak
of all matters according to their hierarchical rank for the good of
the human creature, in both body and soul. Thus he speaks of
Paradise and of the virtues to be pursued and the vices to be
shunned. And because he places vice beside virtue and hell beside   [71]
heaven, he is the better able to reveal the beauty of the one and
the ugliness of the other. Moreover, he simply follows the work
begun by Guillaume de Lorris when he mentions the act of love
in the chapter of Jealousy, of the Old Woman, and in various other
places. Genius does not grant Paradise to foolish lovers, as Lady
Eloquence suggests, but rather to those who perform the works of
nature virtuously. There is a vast difference between performing
the works of nature virtuously and being a foolish lover. Neither
Nature nor Genius exhort a man to be a foolish lover; rather,
they preach that one ought to follow the works of nature. To
propagate the human species and to abhor the sin against nature
— these are the legitimate aims which they propose. And although
I do not dare, and do not wish, to say that it is not sinful, outside
the state of marriage, to perform the work of nature for the two
above-mentioned reasons, nevertheless I dare say that it *is* permitted
within marriage; and this is Master Jean de Meun's point in the
chapter of the Old Woman. For this reason marriages are made

> By the advice of wise men ...   [13916]

> In order to prevent arguments,
> Contentions and murders,
> And in order to aid in rearing children,
> Who are their joint responsibility.   [13891-4]

By God, this is not to cast aspersions on marriage! I say that
marriage was ordained by wise men, but I will tell you what
St. Augustine says concerning marriage in the book of his *Confessions*: "It is good for a man not to touch a woman," and "the
man who is not married thinks of divine things to please God, but
the married man thinks of secular things to please his wife." [24] I
will call this passage to your mind and to all others who wish to

---

[24] *Confessions,* II.ii. Augustine quotes here I Corinthians VII.1 and I
Corinthians VII.32-33.

criticize unreasonably an author who is famous and who has not
previously been criticized, although perhaps your friend is more
familiar with Augustine than I. But there is none so deaf as he
who will not hear.

It seems then that the work of nature is permissible in some
cases, that it is not evil in itself, but rather by some consequence.
For the work of nature is permissible at least in marriage, and thus
Genius encouraged men to do the work of nature for the two
purposes I mentioned by granting Paradise to those who perform
it virtuously and refrain from vice. For these are his own words. I   [72]
do not see an error there at all. And because everyone has not
read the book of the *Rose,* I will quote here the words of Genius
himself, and may I be pardoned if I am too prolix in quoting now
and at other times the very words of the book. I do it for two
reasons: first, that no one will think that I say something which
is not in the book, because there are many who have not read it
at all, as I have said; the other reason is that I could not express
an idea as briefly in prose as Master Jean de Meun says it in
leonine rime. Here then are the words of Genius:

> He who strives to love well
> Without any ignoble thought
> And loyally puts himself to the task
> May he go garlanded with flowers into paradise;
> And if he has made a good confession
> I will take upon myself all his deeds
> With all the power that I can muster.   [19535-41]

And in order to recapitulate his sermon, he says:

> Think how to honor Nature,
> Serve her will by working well   [20637-8]
> ... ...
> And if you have the goods of another,
> Return them if you can,
> And if you cannot
> Because you have spent or gambled them away,
> Remember them when you
> Later have plenty of goods.
> Stay away from murder
> Keep your hand and lips clean,
> Be loyal and compassionate,
> Then you will go into the Delightful Field
> By following the path of the lamb.   [20639-49]

This is in brief the recapitulation of Genius' whole sermon and the message that he had previously given. After you and those who criticize him have read this clear message completely, why do you not pay heed to it? Thus I cannot marvel enough how anybody dares to blame him — I mean not only him but all those who prize and love his book of the *Rose*. As for myself, in good truth, I had rather be among the blamed and scorned for prizing and loving the book of the *Rose* than to be among its blamers and reproachers. And may all those who reproach him know well, that seven thousand remain who will never bend the knee before Baal,[25] and who are full ready to defend him. If he were contemporary with you who blame him, I would say that you have particular hatred for him personally, but you have never so much as seen him. Thus I cannot imagine whence this comes, save that the very loftiness of the book invites the winds of Envy. Your ignorance is not at all the cause of this criticism; this did not come certainly from your sketchy reading of the book of the *Rose*. Perhaps you merely pretend to blame the said book in order to exalt it, that is, by causing your hearers to read it. And you know well that he who reads it will find there much worthy teaching, the opposite of your criticism. And if this is your intent, you and the critics of the work should be held excused. For such purpose would be good, whatever the means. Yet I pray you, woman of high intellect, that you preserve the honor you have won for the depth of your understanding and elegant style; and if men have praised you for having, as it were, fired a shot over the towers of Notre Dame, do not attempt to hit the moon with a cannon ball. Take care not to be like the crow who, because someone praised his song, began to sing louder than usual and let his mouthful fall. And at all events, I pray all men and women who wish to criticize or blame him in any part to read him thoroughly first, four times at least,

[73]

---

25 Particularly problematic, for modern scholar as for medieval scribe, is the distinction between the MS. *ung* and *vij.* That *seven* is the number meant here is assured by the biblical text, Romans XI.4: "I have left me seven thousand men that have not bowed their knees to Baal." When Rose Rigaud (*Les Idees feministes de Christine de Pisan,* p. 63) writes that, if we were to believe Pierre Col, seven thousand of his contemporaries were ready to take up the pen in defense of Jean de Meun, she has simply failed to recognize the biblical quotation. We are, in fact, indebted to Erik Hicks for calling it to our attention.

that they may the better understand him. And I will accept such
a thorough reading for their absolution. If they decline to do this,
let them at least consider the purpose for which he wrote his
book, and let them read his justification without prejudice, and I
am sure that they will excuse him, for there is no other justification
or response necessary than the one that he himself put directly
before the beginning of the assault. For there and only there does
he speak as author, and there, as author, he says:

> For nobody ought to despise a woman,
> Unless he has the wickedest of all possible hearts.
> [15209-10]

> And he protests
> That it is not his intention
> To speak against any living man,
> Following holy religion,
> Or leads his life in good works,
> Whatever his cloak.   [15251-6]

[74]

And

> If he uses words
> That are too bawdy or foolish,   [15161-2]
> His subject matter required them,
> And made him use such expressions,   [15173-4]

because of the inherent nature of the matter itself, and besides he
does nothing more than quote there anyway. And generally he says
that he has never said anything which was not for instruction, that
is, for each one to have knowledge of himself and others. And
finally:

> That if he has said any word
> Which Holy Church considers foolish,   [15299-300]

he is completely ready to amend it.

I am greatly amazed when I hear such words of criticism against
this book put in the mouth of Lady Theological Eloquence and of

the entire Court of Holy Christianity,[26] when they have let the book lie undisturbed for the space of one hundred years or more; and particularly so now that the book has been published throughout all Christendom and even translated into foreign languages. But I believe that they have waited for you — you and others who wish to criticize him. For I know of a truth that previously there has been nobody who saw fit to reproach him. Witness, for example, the four mendicant orders, among whom there have been very notable clerks who had no small influence with the Pope, as well as with temporal princes and princesses, and he was not particularly indulgent toward them. Now, consider what a promoter Conscience was, who allowed such a cause to lie dormant for a hundred years — by the body of God! One does little honor certainly to all of this Holy Court of Christianity to attribute to it such negligence, and especially to Lady Theological Eloquence, who adopts a poor line of argument for her case and presents it badly by arguing it in the manner which the masters of rhetoric have laid down in their books, a method which is not appropriate to theological eloquence, as St. Augustine says in the fourth book of *De Doctrina Christiana*. For God's sake, they wished Lady Eloquence to take on a thankless task, without giving her any aid. But I know well their response. They will say they had hardly thought [75] of it. Nevertheless, I ask all this blessed Court that they forgive the one who has imposed on them such a character. For I know certainly that he had a good purpose, namely the same as Master Jean de Meun's. It is true that *I* could scarcely forgive him for the misdeed of imputing to them such negligence and involving them in such a pointless quarrel, even though he did not do it through malice. For I believe that there is in him no malice at all, or as little as in any man living. But his error arose only from the fact that he had little read this noble book of the *Rose,* and did not grasp that little that he did read. Deign to pardon him then, Lady Canonical Justice, Reason, Eloquence, Conscience, and the

---

[26] Col has apparently forgotten that, in condemning Christine's hasty judgment, he had praised Gerson for leaving the decision suspended in the Court of Christianity.

other barons of the Holy Court of Christianity, and impose on him as penance for his offence, that he read in its entirety and without haste this most noble book of the Rose, three times in honor of the blessed Trinity in unity. And may the Trinity grant us all a fleece so white that we may, with the said de Meun, crop the grass which grows in the park of the little gamboling lamb.[27] Amen.

[76]

---

27 Cf. Roman de la Rose, 19935-39.

XIV

CHRISTINE DE PISAN'S REPLY TO PIERRE COL

*[This, the longest letter in the debate, is Christine's point-by-point
answer to Pierre Col's preceding letter. She dates the letter
herself: October 2, 1402. The Old French text is to be found
in Ward, pp. 83-111.]*

To M. Pierre Col, Secretary of the King our Lord.

Because human understanding cannot attain to a perfect knowledge of absolute truth and cannot comprehend mysteries on account
of the gross, terrestrial darkness which impedes and obstructs true
light, so that men draw conclusions from opinion rather than from
certain knowledge — for these reasons, debates often arise among
even the wisest of men because of differing opinions, each one
striving to show by his reasoning that his particular opinion is the
true one. That this is true can be seen from our present debate.
Therefore, O wise clerk, whose keen feeling and facility in ex-
pressing your opinions are impeded by no ignorance, I wish to
inform you that, although your reasons are well laid out for your
purpose, they are contrary to my belief. For despite your beautiful
rhetoric, you do not move my heart at all or make me wish to
change what I have previously written. On this matter which your
recent letter dealt with, namely the debate begun some time ago
over the *Roman de la Rose,* I have received and been encouraged
by writings addressed to me by other important people. And
although I am otherwise engaged and did not intend to write more
on the subject, I will nevertheless answer you, bluntly and directly
according to my custom, and speak the truth without any glossing

over. And since I did not know how to emulate your good style, may you take into consideration my lack of skill.

Your letter began by saying that just when you were anxious to see my writings, you came into the possession of a certain letter of mine addressed to Monsignor Provost of Lisle, which began: "Reverence, honor, etc." Then immediately you affirm that I make an effort to reproach this exalted Catholic, divine orator, etc., Master Jean de Meun, in some particular parts of the book of the *Rose.* In the praise of this work, you say, "you would not dare to open your mouth nor advance your foot and step into an abyss." [83] Mother of God! Let us pause here a moment. Is he then equal to Jesus Christ or to the Virgin Mary; is he greater than St. Paul or the doctors of Holy Church, whom you say you could not praise sufficiently even if all your members were changed into tongues, etc. Nevertheless, it is true (saving your grace) that too extreme and excessive praise given to a creature occasions reproach and turns to blame. And although I would gradly remain silent — for the matter does not please me — pure truth constrains me to answer you, and I will do so in my unpolished style. You asked me, also, to pardon you for addressing me familiarly by "tu," and I request the same of you, because, as you said, the ancients felt that this was the most appropriate form.

First of all, you declare that I condemn without grounds the fact that Reason, in the chapter devoted to her in the *Roman de la Rose,* names the secret members of man by their proper names. Then you repeat my previous objection to this, namely, that God truly created all things good, but by the pollution of our first parents' sin man became impure; and that Lucifer was first given a beautiful name, but later was transformed into a horrible person; and, finally, that the name does not make the thing dishonorable, but the thing, the name. By saying this, I resemble, you say, the pelican, which kills itself with its beak. This was your conclusion. Then you go on to say that if the thing, therefore, makes the name dishonorable, what name can one give to the thing which would not be dishonorable? Without more ado, I will answer this bluntly, for I am no logician. To be honest, there is no need for such rationalizations. Indeed, I do admit to you that, because of corrupted will, I could in no way speak of a dishonorable thing, whether the secret members or some other ignoble matter, whatever name I should give them, without the name becoming dishonorable. Nevertheless, if in the case of sickness or some other need, it were necessary to refer specifically to the secret members or whatever else, and if, in such a situation, I were able to make myself clearly understood by using some other name, then I would not at all be speaking dishonorably. The reason is that the purpose for which I spoke in that case would not be dishonorable. Yet, even in such a case, if I were to name them by their proper names, I would indeed be speaking dishonorably, for the primary associations of [84] the thing have already made the name dishonorable.

It follows that my first proposition — that the thing makes the name dishonorable and not the name, the thing — is true. Then you pose the question whether I would speak of, or indeed dare to name, the secret members of a small child, who is innocent, since he is unpolluted by sin. Yet I answer you with this question: I ask you, in reply, whether a small child is brought back again to the same innocence and is in an equal state, not more or less, with Adam when God created him? If you say yes, it is false; for the small child dies painfully, even before he has sinned. And this was not at all true of Adam in the State of Innocence, for from his sin death was born. If you say no, then I say to you that my proposition was true, that such shame was born to us by the pollution of our first parents. And your statement that it is pointless to return to the question of original sin, since it resulted from disobedience is, I admit, accurate. But you say to me, if the pollution of our first parents made the name of the secret members dishonorable, for a stronger reason then one should never call our first parents by name, for they are the ones who sinned and not the members. My response will be this serious problem, which I would be glad to have you solve for me. Why was it that as soon as our first parents had sinned and had knowledge of good and evil, they hid their secret members immediately and became ashamed, although they had not yet made use of them? I ask you why they did not cover their eyes or their mouths, with which they had sinned, rather than their secret members? It seems to me that at that moment reasonable shame was born, which you and your accomplices, as well as the character your master named Reason, wish to hunt down and destroy. Thus it seems to me that I am not at all killed by my own beak, as you have asserted.

I am far from alone in the true, just, and reasonable opinion which I hold against the work of the *Rose* on account of its most reprehensible lessons, although there may well be some good in it. Among the other good people who agree with me, a courageous teacher and master of theology — competent, worthy, admirable, estimable, elect among the elect — came forward, after I had written the letter which you say you have seen. Having decided to increase virtue and destroy vice (with which the work of the *Rose* has poisoned many human hearts) by opposing that book, he composed a short work, clearly inspired by pure theology.[1] Concerning this matter, you wrote me that you have seen a work "made in the manner of a Complaint in the Holy Court of Christianity, in which Canonical Justice was established as judge, and the virtues around her as her council, the chief and chancellor of which was Wise Understanding, accompanied by Lady Reason, Prudence, Knowledge, and others as secretaries. Theological Eloquence was advocate of the Court. The promoter of the suits was Conscience, who brought up and presented a request by Chastity, as follows: 'To Justice the law giver, who holds the place of God on earth, and to the universal Court of his devout and most Christian religion, Chastity, your faithful subject, humbly supplicates and requests that you provide a remedy and a brief warning against the intolerable deeds which a certain Foolish Lover has been doing and continues to do to me,' and he places thereafter eight or nine articles."

[85]

You begin the aforementioned letter by addressing me alone, since you consider it easy to repudiate my reasoning on account of my ignorance, because, apparently, you are confident of your own good sense and subtlety. Then, inexplicably, you begin voicing your personal criticism of the words of the abovementioned notable person in his well written work, since his opinion is contrary to your own erroneous one. Now consider well, consider well whether I might not reasonably apply to you the insulting words which you addressed to me in some places, saying: "Oh outrageous presumption! Oh excessively foolish pride!" etc. It is not at all my intention, however, to take upon myself the defense of all the ques-

---

[1] This is merely the middle of an exceedingly complicated Old French sentence, which because of its often elliptical structure, is difficult to translate. Apparently to indicate a gap in the sense, Ward twice used marks of ellipsis — not justified by the MSS.— within this one long sentence.

tions posed by Lady Eloquence, for these are not related to the purpose of my first letter, save in a few places which raise the subject you would re-argue with me. For I will defer to the man who wrote the said Complaint, since he would be better able to defend it in a few words than I could in an entire lifetime. But I can say this much about the matter: you wish, unreasonably, to accuse him of ignorance — you who think you understand the work better than he, for all his wisdom and deep learning. You say indeed (to speak more courteously about such a notable person) that if he had studied the said book well, just as his understanding towers over all others, so too would his praise and appreciation of it. Praised be God! how good it must be to presume to believe, as you do, that such a man (who, you admit, is a worthy person) would have publicly condemned a work, before he had even completely understood it!   [86]

Further, I can easily answer what you said about his speaking as a scholar about the Foolish Lover, and therefore as one who had never felt the effect of foolish love. It is never necessary to have experience of a thing in order to speak properly of it. And many examples of this could be given to you, as you well know. Subtle things too numerous for one man to experience and even beyond natural experience have been accurately described, so that the effects of love are not incomprehensible to a man of keen understanding. You yourself admit that it is not necessary to have experience. Nevertheless, you conclude that if he had had the experience of a foolish lover, he would have spoken differently.

I pass over in this place some articles of the abovementioned complaint of Lady Eloquence, because they are not for me to answer, nor will I discuss your remark about what Master Jean de Meun called sanctuaries, for silence is safest. But because you excuse him and say that they can be legitimately called by that name in order to demonstrate the folly of the Foolish Lover, certainly you are not saying what you think, begging your pardon. For you know well that he never said it with the intention that the thing could be called holy, but rather as a kind of exciting derision, more stimulating for lecherous men. At least, whatever his intention, I know well that he sounds evil to people who do not delight in such carnality.

I do not wish to neglect your point that I ought not to think "what he says in his *Testament* — 'I have made in my youth many works through vanity' — refers to the book of the Rose." You speak as if you had certain knowledge that he never did repent of it and that he did not use these words because of such repentance. Yet, nonetheless, he did not make an exception of it in any way. But you say that he meant ballades, rondeaux, and virelais that have not come down to us. Where then are these other vain and foolish works that he wrote? It is marvelous that these works of such a sovereign writer have not been carefully preserved, for [87] many references have been made to the works of other men who could not be compared to him; whereas there is no one alive who has ever heard of those other works of his. I myself have often wondered that so great a writer produced so little work, though it is true, many of his devotees wished to attribute to him even works by St. Augustine. Nevertheless, if you imply that he did not mention them in order to avoid vainglory, but that he did, in fact, write several, look in the prologue to his translation of Boethius, where he enumerates his original works and translations: I don't believe that he forgot a single one. I say this for the benefit of those who wish to attribute other writings to him, although I do not wish to be involved in that matter. But, to return to our subject, I am firmly convinced that the words of his testament refer strictly to this romance, for this is apparent in his words, and we know nothing to the contrary.

You return to my point and say that Lady Eloquence says: " 'Is this not,' says she, 'great madness to say that one ought to speak bluntly and crudely and without shame, however dishonorable the words in the judgment of all people.' " Then you say to Lady Eloquence that she has been made to present her original premise badly and that it is upon this that she bases all her subsequent argument. But then you excuse her creator by accusing him of ignorance and, as I have said before, you say that it is your belief that he has badly read and inadequately studied the book.

In making your response to Lady Eloquence you quote from the *Roman de la Rose* Reason's words, which say essentially that she can indeed name things by their proper names, whether they are good or not. And you say Jean de Meun does not argue there that one has to name them but that one may do so. On behalf of

Lady Eloquence, I will reply to you somewhat bluntly. I know
perfectly well that duty is constraint and power is will, but nonetheless one's choice of words in such a case can make an offense
of speaking openly and fully, as has already been proved and will
be again. Yet you maintain, along with Reason, that one can speak
of them by their proper names without sin, and you even allege
that the Bible and holy writings name them by their proper names,
where it is appropriate. I answer you, good friend, that if the
Bible or holy writings name them, the manner of speaking and
the purpose are entirely different from his work; rather, their aim
is far removed from carnal enticement. The Bible certainly is not
the work of a female character who called herself the daughter of   [88]
God, and it never speaks to a Foolish Lover in order to fan the
fires of lust. You say, moreover, that if the name displeases some
people, it does not, certainly, displease all, and I quite believe you
in this remark, for something evilly done and said never displeases
everybody. And you say that your remark stems from Lady Eloquence's comment that the words are so very dishonorable in the
opinion of all people. Here, when you say that one ought not to
take the words according to the letter, you entangle yourself in
the little cord with which you thought to catch me. For you know
very well that the greatest part is taken for the whole, and truly
the majority of people would be displeased to hear dishonorable
things named publicly. You say that there is no case for claiming
that good custom forbids speaking thus plainly, a subject which
you do not discuss further. Yet I do not see why you will not
speak to the matter whether the custom is good or evil, if you
know something good about it. But you report Lady Eloquence as
saying that if one thinks the custom is evil, he assumes foolishly
that women have never accustomed themselves to it. Yet she is
right. And it would be a pity if it were otherwise and if such a
reproach could be brought by other countries against the women
of this kingdom. For as it is said in the common proverb, "By the
tongue, the inclination is known." For even Reason whom you hold
as so great an authority says that this has never been customary
in France. And indeed it has not been the custom. For never have
they acustomed themselves to it; and why not? This comes about
from reasonable shame, which (thanks be to God) they have never
lost. Then you say that it is possible that in other countries ladies

call them by name. But I don't understand why you say such a
thing when you know nothing about it, and nobody has ever said
that women and men anywhere speak thus plainly and publicly.
You say that you are amazed at the custom of women's naming
their own secret members by their proper names, while refusing to
name a man's. I answer you that (saving your grace) certainly
honorable women do not say the name publicly; and if some women
name the things which are private to them more than those which
are not, you ought not to be astonished. But you who assert by so
many arguments that Master Jean de Meun's Reason is right in
saying that they should be called openly by name, I ask you sincerely, you who are his very especial disciple as you say, why you
do not name them openly in your own writing without beating
around the bush? It seems to me that you are not a good pupil,
for you do not follow well at all the doctrine of your master, who
teaches you to name them. If you say that this is not customary,   [89]
are you then afraid of being criticized, so that you take heed to
this custom? Do you wish to live by the opinion of other people?
Rather, follow good doctrine, in order to show them what they
ought to do, for all things must begin somewhere. And if someone
blames you at first, you will be praised for it later, when people
see that the custom is good and right. Ha! my God! you do not
do so. You cannot deny that shame keeps you from it. And where
is Master Jean de Meun's Reason? She has little power when
shame defeats her. Blessed be such shame that defeats such Reason.
If I hated you, I would say, would to God that you had gone
against custom in this matter. But I love you for your good sense
and the good that people say of you. Although I scarcely know
you, I do not wish you the dishonor of speaking frankly. For honorable and virtuous speech is the mark of a praiseworthy person.

It seems to me that you condemn Lady Eloquence's argument
that Meun observed the rules of rhetoric badly, in that he failed
to consider to whom Reason was speaking. For, she maintains,
Reason spoke to a Foolish Lover, who would simply be more
inflamed by her words. And this would not be true of a learned
man, since a philosopher or a theologian could not be a lover, a
fact which you deny, citing the examples of David, Solomon, and
others. Yet I am amazed that you wish to correct in others that
very fault into which you yourself have fallen. And you uphold

at one point what you wish to refute at another. It is good to
know that when the gallant gentleman spoke of the Foolish Lover
he assumed that this man was completely ignorant; in the case of
foolish love, he presumed that there was great knowledge in it;
and when he said "A great theological clerk," he assumed that the
passion of foolish love was not in him. For it is fitting that his
fine intellect which makes no mistakes should conceive it in this
way or even more subtly! But you say that a man will not be
influenced by such words to love foolishly, and the reply is that
he is already influenced, since he is a foolish lover. But his passion
can indeed be increased. You say that when Reason named them,
she preached to the Lover that he should refrain completely from
foolish love. My answer. If this is true, as Master Jean de Meun
holds and you believe, it is not the general rule, one might argue,
to strive so hard for such a purpose! Reason did by the Lover
just as if I were to speak to a pregnant woman or an invalid and   [90]
were to describe to him the pleasures of tart apples, fresh pears,
or other fruit, which would be enticing but harmful to him, and
as if I were to say to him that if he would eat of them, it would
be greatly harmful to him. I believe, certainly, that his memory
would have been sharpened and his appetite whetted more by the
naming of the things than by the command not to eat them. And
this is a good example of the kind of thing I am talking about.
Yet you strongly condemn what I said about not reminding human
nature of the foot on which it limps! You argue that Master Jean
de Meun in the chapter on Reason did not forbid speaking of the
secret members on account of his fondness for speaking of them,
but in order to show the foolishness of those who say that it is
not permissible to speak of them. Certainly if he did it for this
reason, he failed in his intention, when he attempted by means of
a very great folly to attain to a very great wisdom. It is clear, you
say, that he did not do it for cupidity, because elsewhere when
he speaks of the work of nature, he calls it the "game of love."
There you have it! Ha! true God! You speak marvels: in the same
way, you could say that at the end of his book he does not name
by their proper names dishonorable things that are there. And,
assuredly, he does not, and what is that worth? He names them
by poetic but nonetheless explicit words which are a hundred times
more enticing and more alluring and more sensual to those who

are inclined in that way, than if he had named them by their proper names. You say, moreover, that whoever reads and understands the said romance will realize that Master Jean de Meun should not have spoken in any other way. Your point is well made, so long as the reader understands it as you do. You know that it happens with the reading of this book as with the books of the alchemists. Some people read them and understand them in one way; others read them and understand them in a totally opposite way. And each thinks he understands very well indeed. As a result they work to prepare furnaces, alembics, and crucibles, mixing together various metals and materials. With great effort, they blow up the fire, and, because of a minute bit of sublime metal or mere residue which seems marvelous to them, they think they have worked wonders. Then after they have worked and worked and wasted their time, they know no more than before, except the cost, expense, and the art of distilling and congealing, knowledge of no value at all. So it is with you and me and many others. You understand the book in one way, and I, quite the opposite. You quote; I reply. And when we have worked and worked, it is all worth nothing. For the matter[2] is very dishonorable, much like certain alchemists who think they can transmute dung. Now it would be best to say nothing more about the matter, and I would prefer not to be an alchemist in this affair, but I must defend myself since I have been attacked. [91]

With regard to your next argument criticising Lady Eloquence's complaint before Justice against Jean de Meun, I will leave it to the writer of that Complaint to answer, for he will know how to answer well when he chooses.

You repeat my earlier comment that I cannot help marveling at Reason's statement that in the amorous war it is better to deceive than to be deceived. And you say that I argue that it would thus follow that both things would then be good — which cannot be. Then you swear your oath that it would have been to my honor if I had not put such an argument in writing, and that such a contention is like children's propositions when they argue. Nevertheless, whatever you think of it, I assure you of this: I have no

---

[2] Christine is surely punning on "la matiere." See page xvii of the Introduction.

intention of withdrawing it. To your effort at undermining my argument by citing Jesus Christ's words that it would have been better for Judas not to have been born than to have betrayed his master, I reply that indeed it was good that Jesus Christ died, and it was good that Judas was born. But it would have been better for him indeed, if he had never been born, on account of his despair and the punishment for his betrayal. And you yourself have not consistently followed the rule which you use to criticize me. You, in fact, interpret in an extraordinary way what is said clearly and literally. "It is far better, dear master, to deceive than to be deceived," which clearly, according to your view, means that it would harm you less to make a semblance of loving me in order to enjoy my body, than if you lost thereby your "learning, sense, time, soul, body, and reputation"! This is most extravagantly spoken. From this it appears that it is necessary to deceive or to lose "sense, time, soul," etc. Certainly your prejudice in favor of Meun makes you go a long way to seek this extreme justification. Nevertheless, he by no means puts these two extremities together. Thus I say and say again that in the law of Jesus Christ and according to his doctrine, it is more strictly forbidden to deceive one's neighbor than to be deceived. I mean, of course, fraudulent deceit, for, loosely speaking, there is such a thing called deceit which is not a great vice at all. But lest I forget, I will say now   [92] what does please me in your remarks: that is, that you believe Master Jean de Meun never wrote this in his book at all, but that it was interpolated. It seems clear that you say this because you wish it to be so (saving your grace), for this passage is in the same language and the same style, but you wish very much that he had never said it. You can right boldly say that such words were never uttered by Reason, the daughter of God!

Ha! fraudulent deception! mother of treason! who is this who dares to advance you in any circumstance? And since we have entered into the matter (before God!), let me, despite the prolixity, stay with it a moment, because one cannot completely understand many things in a short time. By your faith, reflect a bit, you who have read history! What vice has held, and still holds, a greater place in this world, in aiding and abetting the most extreme perversities? You will find it to be deceit. Was it not deceit that bequeathed death to us in the first place? Think about it. Read the

Trojan histories. In Ovid and others, you will discover how Lady Discord sowed the seed of that war. But she would never have reaped the harvest, had not Lady Deceit intervened, by causing the betrayal and capture of the fortress of Troy. That story is full of her countless misdeeds. Ha! God! Every noble heart ought to guard itself against harboring so heinous a vice, beyond all others! What distinction do you make between treachery and deceit? I know of none at all, save that the one sounds worse than the other. And if you say that it is better to rely on another than to have another rely on you, I answer immediately that this is not true. For according to the justice of God, he who injures another is punished more severely than the one who is injured. And the same is true, let us point out, in the case of love; yet Master Jean de Meun's Reason says that "It is better," etc. Anyway, I will tell you my opinion, and whoever wishes to do so can call me a fool. Ha! deceit! I have an only son (God preserve him!), and I wish for him that he be thoroughly in love, while at the same time preserving the good sense which all reasonable men have and which I hope God will grant him. May he be blessed with a well-bred and prudent wife, who will love and honor him — it has happened before and could well happen for him. I would much prefer this than that he should be capable of deceiving many or all women. For I believe that by deceiving many, he could more quickly lose [93] "sense, time, soul, body, and reputation," than by loving only one woman well. And do you think that I believe as you do that to be a lover is the worst mischief that can happen to a young man, when this is in its proper place, honorable and sensible? For he who would love a shepherdess must be ready to watch the sheep. I do not say this on account of the station, but of the condition, in order to show that the loving heart always desires to conform to the customs of the one he loves. Therefore, I firmly believe that those who wish to love ought to choose carefully where they will place their affections. For there, I believe, lies the peril. Yet you think I believe that all those who have been, or are now, lovers find all their happiness in striving to bed their ladies. Certainly, I do not at all believe this. For I am sure that many lovers, whose main intent was that their morals should be enhanced by their ladies, have loved loyally and perfectly without ever going to bed with them and without ever deceiving, or being deceived by them.

And by virtue of this love, they became valiant and famous, so much so, in fact, that in their old age they praised God that they had been lovers. And I have heard it said that this opinion was held even by the good constable My Lord Bertrand du Guesclin, My Lord Morise de Trisguidi, [3] and many other knights. And they never lost "sense, time, soul, body, and reputation." I speak so much of this reputation, because you have written me that I should mark it well. Now, I have marked it well for you. At this point, you gave several answers, saying that Master Jean de Meun had in mind those who were excessively foolish in love. I answer that even good things can be used badly. But since he wished to describe love fully, he should not have so narrowly restricted himself to a single purpose, certainly not to a purpose so dishonorably described. You will say to me that I contradict Lady Eloquence,   [94] who speaks of the Foolish Lover whom Meun mentions, and I say to you that being a lover does not necessarily mean being foolish, and that one does not have to lose "sense, time," etc., on account of love. You will further say to me that I encourage the young to be lovers. I say to you that I do not really approve of their being such, for all earthly love is mere vanity. But if one of the two is necessary, it is worse to deceive than to be a lover; and worse things can come from it. But because Master Jean de Meun, who described many things very well, never did describe the essential quality of the deceiver, I will speak of it a little in rude style, in order to whet the appetite of those who take delight in such things. The deceiver is a liar, perjurer, hypocrite, flatterer, traitor, and a covert agitator; he is false and malicious, the cause of boundless evil. And finally when you can think of nothing further, he is a scandalous mocker, an envious and suspicious man — these are his titles. But to repeat your judgment against the man who composed the above-mentioned complaint that he did not understand what a foolish lover was, I can declare, because I have spoken about those who love honorably, that Master Jean de Meun did not understand what an honorable lover was.

---

3 Bertrand du Guesclin (1320-1380). Constable of Charles V and his principal assistant in the wars against England, he was the exemplar of the perfect knight. Morise de Trisguidi, a Breton, was a retainer of Du Guesclin.

Then you speak of the deep dismay which Lady Eloquence and I express about the great dishonorableness in the chapter of the Old Woman, when we say that one can find nothing there but total filth and vile teaching, and similarly in the chapter of Jealousy. And we say much more that you do not reply to. Then you completely misread my words at the end of my aforementioned letter, remembering this part badly, begging your pardon. For you claim I said that I do not condemn the author or authors in all places in the said book, as if, you say, I meant that I condemned him for those parts which I criticized, charging that I set myself up as judge on the basis of mere opinion. My answer is that, in reality, you have ill chosen the flowers of my writing and have made a clumsily arranged bouquet, saving your grace. It was not by opinion but by certain knowledge that I declared that he spoke in a gross and most dishonorable manner in several places and generally gave an evil exhortation. This judgment is easy to make, for it is proved by the work itself. Thus you or I or anyone else who understands [95] French can condemn him on this point. Yet because he does not speak so dishonorably throughout, I say that I do not condemn him throughout. Further, you report correctly my wishing I could find someone to explain to me how so many dishonorable things could be good. And, nevertheless, you do not provide this explanation, but rather pass over it without fulfilling the wish. And since you are angry with me without reason, you attack me harshly with, "Oh outrageous presumption! Oh excessively foolish pride! Oh opinion uttered too quickly and thoughtlessly by the mouth of a woman! A woman who condemns a man of high understanding and dedicated study, a man who, by great labor and mature deliberation, has made the very noble book of the Rose, which surpasses all others that ever were written in French. When you have read this book a hundred times, provided you have understood the greater part of it, you will discover that you could never have put your time and intellect to better use! " My answer. Oh man deceived by wilful opinion! I could assuredly answer but I prefer not to do it with insult, although, groundlessly, you yourself slander me with ugly accusations. Oh darkened understanding! Oh perverted knowledge blinded by self will, which judges grievous poison to be restoration from death; perverse doctrine to be healthful example; bile to be sweet honey; horrible filthiness to be satisfying beauty.

A simple little housewife sustained by the doctrine of Holy Church could criticize your error! Flee and eschew the perverse doctrine which could lead you to damnation. When God has once enlightened you with true knowledge, you will be horrified by it, when you turn around and look back down the dangerous path you travelled.

You say in order to reprove me that truth engenders hatred and flattery friends, as Terence says. [4] And on account of this, you suspect that I wish to bite him, and counsel me to watch my teeth. Know this for a certainty, that you lack somewhat in your thinking there (saving your reverence), for because there are so many deceiving lies and lack of truth in the book, I wish not only to bite, but to pull up by the roots the very great fallacious lies which it contains. You respond to Lady Eloquence and me that Master Jean de Meun introduced characters in his book, and made each one   [96] speak fittingly, according to what pertained to him. I readily admit that the proper equipment is necessary for any particular game, but the will of the player manipulates such equipment to his own purpose. And it is clearly true (may it not displease you) that he was at fault in attributing to some of his characters functions which do not properly belong to them: as with his priest he calls Genius, who insistently commands men to bed the ladies and to continue the work of nature without leaving off. And yet he then has Genius say that one ought to flee women above all things, accusing them of as much evil and villainy as possible. I do not understand how it pertains to his office or even to the function of many other characters who say the same. You say that it is the role of the Jealous Man to speak in such a way; my reply is that never, in all his characters, can Meun resist the temptation to slander women viciously. They are, thanks to God, none the worse for this. But, anyway, in my other letter, I spoke of this matter fully, to which remarks you scarcely responded, a fact which leaves me hardly anything to say.

Since this book of the *Rose* is so necessary and so important for teaching the good moral life, tell me, pray, what benefit to the common good can come from a collection of such immoral lessons as those espoused by the character called the Old Woman.

---

[4] *Andria,* 68.

For if you say that Meun's purpose is to teach men to guard themselves from these evils, I reply that most people, I believe, have never had anything to do with the kind of devilment that she describes and do not even know that such things exist. Therefore, from innocence like this, no harm can befall the general good, when most people are unaware of such evil in the first place. After you have read his words, which do you yourself remember more clearly, I would dearly like to know, the goodness of a chaste and virtuous life or the dissoluteness of the expressions? It is marvellous how you, his allies, have, by your interpretation, turned such horrible evil into such great good. Likewise, with regard to the Jealous Man, you say that he speaks merely as a jealous man. I reply, as I did of the Old Woman, that there was indeed great need for this wasteful display of crude words to enhance the common good! Your weak explanation why the Jealous Man says so much evil of women is not to my purpose; therefore, I pass over it. [97]

Moreover, you reply to Lady Eloquence and me, by asking whether a man's citing of the crime reported by another can lead a person to commit the same crime, as, for example, Sallust's account of the Catiline conspiracy against the Roman republic, or Aristotle's quotation of the erroneous opinions of ancient philosophers? Is, therefore, Holy Scripture, which recounts the abominable sins of Sodom and Gomorrah, guilty of exhorting men to commit such sins? You speak very well and to the point, you believe, but I ask you whether these authors or Holy Scripture itself, in recounting such things, makes use of invented characters or soft, alluring words which support and sustain treachery, heresy, and other evils? You know very well that it is not so, for wherever such evils are recounted in books, they are condemned in such a way that they sound unpleasant to all who hear. And you used the example of the preacher's calling to mind in his sermon the foot on which one limps, because I had said previously that one need not remind nature of this, in order to make her walk straighter. But how does he call it to mind? How? Does he say "My children, play! rejoice! take your ease — do so; this is the way to paradise! " By God, my lord, he does not; rather, he calls to mind this foot in such a way that it horrifies the hearers. One could say, "God grant you good day," in such a way that it sounds evil and bitter.

Then you complain to Chastity, saying, "Ha, Lady, is this the praise you wish to give to Master Jean de Meun, who has valued you and all other virtues to highly, and blamed all vices that the understanding can conceive?" "Yes," you say, "as human understanding can conceive! " And then afterward you say that I should not smirk about it. Ha! How well you knew that I would laugh at this good word! For when I think of the beautiful teachings and honorable words of Chastity, I have good reason for laughing at what you said. Then you say afterward that whoever reads the book thoroughly "will find there exhortation to flee all vices and to pursue all virtues," and then you give some teaching which you claim it contains. I tell you frankly that you could do the same with the law of Mohammed. If you read the Koran, you will find in it some very good and moral points of our faith, which will please you greatly. The work as a whole, however, has been con- [98] demned, and in its entirety is worth nothing. His efforts were completely fruitless, since a work stands or falls by its conclusion. Do you not know that even in council, whatever may have been previously said, people rely on the closing argument. And I dare to say that if Master Jean de Meun had spoken throughout his book of the inclinations and evil conduct of human nature but had concluded in favor of the moral way of life, then you would have had a greater reason for saying that he did it for a good purpose. For you know that if a writer wishes to use rhetoric properly, he first announces his premises and afterward moves from point to point, touching subjects as he chooses, but then always returns, in his conclusion, to the purpose of his narrative. And in this case the author certainly did not fail in any of this in the said book, for its fault is not ignorance. But you will tell me that de Lorris caused this. My answer. I consider the work as a single entity, a fact which is sufficient answer in this regard, although you say many things to suit your purpose, which I pass over, for the whole work comes to a single purpose in the conclusion, interpret as you will.

You have said before that he does not blame women, but rather speaks well of them. But I am waiting for the proof. And you say that St. Ambrose blamed the feminine sex more than he did, for he says that it is a sex accustomed to deceive. I will answer you in this: you know well that the writings of the theologians, and even the sermons of Jesus Christ himself, made use of a double meaning. Thus is it good to know that St. Ambrose never made such a statement in condemnation of women: I am convinced that the good man blamed only vice. For he knew very well that there were many holy women, but he wished to say that it is the feminine sex through which man frequently deceived his own soul, just as Solomon said that the misdeed of a man is worth more than the good deed of a woman.[5] We know well that this is not to be taken according to the letter. But in Solomon himself we see an example. The misdeed of a man would have been far better for him. And indeed if he had not been so enamored of women that he worshipped their idols, he might well have seen some good in women. Solomon's statement could also be read as prophecy, as with the misdeed of Judas which was of far greater worth to us than the good deed of a woman, like Judith who killed Holofernes. Then you say something incredible: you assert that I blame women more than he does by saying that if one read the book of the *Rose*   [99] in the presence of queens or princesses, they would be compelled by shame to cover their blushing faces. And then you say, "Why should they blush? It appears that they believe themselves guilty of the vices that the Jealous Man recites of women." Ha! God! how well said and reported this is! You do yourself very little honor in stating things that can be disproved so easily. You have misconstrued my letter in the place where I said the ladies would be compelled to blush. I did not say this because of the words of the Jealous Man but rather because of the horrible things in that most abominable conclusion. It was this which led me to ask what good there can be in a work which cannot be honorably read in the presence of ladies and to declare that they would blush at it. I do not blame them at all; on the contrary, I praise them for having the chaste virtue of shame.

You answer Lady Eloquence's criticism of Meun's attacks and slanders on religion by saying that he has not attacked religion at all. My reply is this, that as a public defamer (saving your grace) he defames religion excessively and without any exception. The good and devout Catholic, who is capable of criticizing wrongdoing, understands this, and I rely upon his opposition, for it is not pertinent to what I said in my first letter. And as you yourself rightly

---

[5] Ecclus. XLII.14.

say, I could tell you that you quote the good words and select from them whatever suits your purpose, while ignoring the bad ones. To Lady Eloquence's complaint that, in teaching one to capture Jealousy's castle, he desired to drive chastity out of all women, you answer, incredibly, that he wished rather to teach the guards how to block the places through which it could be captured or to place better guards there. And then you say that in all manner of wars the assailants have the advantage only when they are well informed. Now let us speak for a moment between us two about wars. [6] I say to you that there are some kinds of wars in which the assailants have the advantage. Do you know when this is? When the captain or general is very malicious and wise in the ways of war and is dealing with a weak and innocent party not accustomed to war. Then there is another point which often injures the defenders, even when they are strong: the treachery or false   [100] flattery by those very people on whom they rely. In such a way, the strong castle of Ilion was captured long ago. Moreover, when a castle is under attack, you cannot advise someone how to block the holes from treachery, since that treachery is so well concealed. Master Jean de Meun teaches how the castle of Jealousy will be attacked and captured. He does nothing at all to help the defenders in closing up the gaps, for he does not speak to them at all and is not on their side. Rather, he aids and abets the assailants in every form of assault. Thus if I were to advise you how to conquer your enemy, this would clearly not be in order for him to guard himself against you. And if you suggest that Meun does not teach it but simply relates how it was captured, I say to you that a man who describes an evil way of making counterfeit money or how someone had done so, he teaches it rightly enough. Hence, I say with certainty that he did it for no other purpose than to admit the assailants.

Afterward, you introduce Ovid's *Art of Love* for your purpose — and you are caught here in your own trap if you would but consider it. And you give further proof of it, for which I am grateful, when you say that he was wrongly exiled for writing it. You say that Ovid wrote the work in Latin, which women did not understand, and that he gave it to the attackers only, in order to

---

[6] Christine herself, of course, wrote a book on the art of war.

teach them how to attack the castle. This was the purpose of his book, and for this very reason he was exiled — without cause, you say — by the very great jealousy of the Roman men. Certainly, it seems to me that if you had been well advised, you would never have brought into the discussion at this point Ovid's *Art of Love* as an excuse for your master. The only way you could have introduced it to good effect would have been to say that it is the basic foundation and principle of this book of the *Rose,* which is the mirror and exemplar of the good and chaste life, which ideas he took from Ovid, who spoke of nothing save chastity. Ha! God! how obvious it is that sheer will has blinded your good sense, when you say that he was exiled without cause. The Romans, who governed all their deeds with excellent judgment, at that time exiled him, wrongfully you say, on account of jealousy. And since you say afterward that Meun put in his book not only Ovid's *Art of Love* but also the work of many other authors, then even by your own reasoning it is proved that Meun speaks to the attackers, just like Ovid from whom he borrowed. But you say that the more diverse the methods of attack he recounts the better he teaches the castle guards the art of defense. Indeed, he is like a man who attacks and tries to kill you (may God preserve you); he merely teaches you how to defend yourself! Such teaching would be priceless, and you ought to thank him for it! At least you cannot deny that he does not teach how to harm the assailants, whatever the strength of the defenders.

[101]

I cannot help returning to your remark that Ovid was exiled without reason through jealousy, when the wise Romans perceived the perverse and poisonous doctrine prepared in order to sow in the hearts of the young the desire for dissoluteness and idleness, as well as the traps readied to deceive, capture, suborn, and undermine the virginity and chastity of their daughters and wives. These Romans had everything to fear from the dissemination of such a doctrine. Then for punishment, more indulgent really than sufficient, they exiled the author of the doctrine. And there is no doubt that they burned his book, where they could find it. But the root of a bad plant always survives. Ha! *Art of Love!* a book badly named! for of love there is nothing. It could well be called the art of falsely and maliciously deceiving women. This is a beautiful doctrine! Is then everything gained by deceiving women well?

Who are women? Who are they? Are they serpents, wolves, lions, dragons, monsters, or ravishing, devouring beasts and enemies to human nature that it is necessary to make an art of deceiving and capturing them? Read then the *Art*. Learn then how to make traps, capture the forts, deceive them, condemn them, attack this castle, take care that no woman escape from you men, and let everything be given over to shame! And, by God! these are your mothers, your sisters, your daughters, your wives, and your sweethearts: they are you yourselves and you yourselves are they. Now deceive them fully, for it is "much better, dear master, to deceive . . . ," etc.

I laugh at your saying that you lent your book of the *Rose* to a foolish lover so that he could free himself from foolish loving. This book helped him so much that you have heard him swear by his faith that it was this that helped him the most in freeing himself. You claim you mention this because of the words at the end of my letter, "How many have become hermits because of it?" My [102] answer. If you had lent to your friend a book of St. Bernard's devotions or some holy legend which demonstrates that there is but one good love in which one ought to set his heart and affections, as Lady Philosophy shows Boethius, or some similar work, then I promise you that you would have done him far more good. But beware lest you have given him the means of withdrawing from the warmth of the sun and throwing himself into a blazing furnace. And I will give you another example without lying, since we are on the "miracles" of the *Roman de la Rose*. Not long ago, I heard one of your familiar companions and colleagues, a man of authority, say that he knew a married man who believed in the *Roman de la Rose* as in the gospel. This was an extremely jealous man, who, whenever in the grip of passion, would go and find the book and read it to his wife; then he would become violent and strike her and say such horrible things as, "These are the kinds of tricks you pull on me. This good, wise man Master Jean de Meun knew well what women are capable of." And at every word he finds appropriate, he gives her a couple of kicks or slaps. Thus it seems clear to me that whatever other people think of this book, this poor woman pays too high a price for it.

So great a prolixity of language annoys me greatly. For since it is annoying to me, I suppose that it must be so also to the readers. But because it is necessary that I reply to the things brought up — otherwise it would not be understandable — it is necessary for me to lengthen my matter. So may I be pardoned for that which gives annoyance.

Further, you cannot keep quiet concerning the Old Woman, and you say that when she speaks to Fair Welcome, she says to him at the beginning: "Do not seek love, but if you choose to dabble in it, I will teach you gladly," etc. And then she says that she preaches to him so that he will not be deceived. My answer. God have mercy! how malicious is this manner of deceiving — to [103] show that whatever one does or says, however evil, is to a good purpose and to a good cause! For he is not so naive that, once he has detected the deceit, he will not guard himself against it. Thus it is necessary to cover it by a ruse; hence, the best method for a malicious deceiver is to begin with a good introduction, the better to accomplish his evil purpose. Therefore, your suggestion is no justification in this case. You say that if he in any way denigrates or defames the feminine sex in the work, he is merely quoting other authors. My answer. I know well that he is not the first to have denigrated women, but he augments what he quotes. You say that this was in order to teach how to guard the castle better. My answer. One should not suppose that to encourage and praise evil is to teach one to guard himself against it. You say that he did it also in order to continue the work of Guillaume de Lorris. My answer. He who chooses to follow a man who has lost his way can hardly be excused if he himself goes astray. You say that in following de Lorris he speaks "of all matters in their hierarchical order for the good of the human creature, in both body and soul." My answer. We do not hear him speak generally of everything according to their order; he speaks of several things inappropriately, to the detriment of body and soul, as has already been proved. You say that for this reason he spoke of paradise and of the virtues to be pursued and the vices to be shunned. My answer. True, but he, in making his characters praise evil doing, turns vices into virtues, as has been said. He also changes virtue into vice by heaping abuse on the holy and approved marriage state, as well as by defaming other estates indiscriminately. Moreover, he speaks evil of paradise, when he says that lechers will go there — this is his meaning, though the words are somewhat disguised. And he does this through Genius' speech who excommunicates by his power (which is nothing) those who do not perform the work of nature. He teaches more particularly the vices than the virtues. You say that it is because he placed vice beside virtue and hell beside paradise that he is able to show the blessedness of the one and the ugliness of the other. My answer. He does not show the blessedness of paradise at all when he says that evil doers will go there. Rather, he brings paradise into the filthy things that he describes in order to give greater authority to his book. But if you wish to hear paradise and hell described more subtly and, theologically, portrayed more advantageously, poetically, and efficaciously, read the book of Dante, or have it explained to you, because it is written splendidly in the Florentine language. Without wishing to displease you, I say that you will find there sounder principles, and you will be better able to profit from it than from that *Roman de la Rose* of yours. It is one hundred times better written; there is, be not offended, no comparison. You say that Genius certainly does not grant paradise to foolish lovers. My answer. The devil made him promise what is not in his power to grant. But you say that Lady Eloquence misinterprets him. For he speaks, you say, of those who perform the works of nature virtuously. My answer. Now you come to my point, thanks be to God! In fact, he does not speak there of good or evil but simply of those who perform the above-mentioned works. And you say, "There is a vast difference between performing the works of nature virtuously and being a foolish lover." My answer. Not once does he speak of performing this task virtuously. But I say to you that it is worse to be lecherous in many places, as he wishes to teach, than to be deeply in love in a single place. You say that Nature and Genius do not encourage people to be foolish lovers, but that they do encourage the performance of these same works, which are permissible to courtly lovers. My answer. Do you then mean to say, since Nature does not preach it, that it is against nature to be deeply in love? This simply is not true, saving your grace. But since he says that the works of nature are permissible to courtly lovers, it would be worth knowing how they should carry out this purpose. You say that the work of nature is intended for the continuance of the human species and the abandonment of the vice that one ought not to name. My answer. It is pointless to debate this, because, thank God, nature does not lack in anything, and it is a foolish

[104]

waste of time to tell water to follow its natural course. And the other sin which he mentions is not widespread, God be praised, in France. It is scarcely necessary to put such words in anybody's mouth. You say that, "although I do not dare, and do not wish, to say that it is not sinful, outside the state of marriage, to perform the said work." I give you these answers, without more ado: God knows you thought it, and another disciple like you dared to say it. But it is necessary to keep quiet about it, and for good reason. [105] Nevertheless, you say this: "Is it permitted in marriage?" My answer. God be praised for it, we know this well. Nevertheless, the book of the Rose, unlike you, does not make this point about marriage in any place. But you say that this is what Master Jean de Meun intended, when he said in the chapter of the Old Woman these words: "For this reason, marriages are made by the advice of wise men," in order to avoid dissension. My answer. You go to great lengths to find an argument for your purpose which was used for quite another purpose. By no means did the Old Woman preach to Fair Welcome about marriage. She made certain not to, and nothing she said leads to a good purpose. And thus I believe that Master Jean de Meun most certainly did not say these words through her in order to praise marriage, for this was never her function. And I remind you that you previously asserted that this was not Meun speaking, but his characters, each in his own role. But here it was he who said this good word! and there it was not he who spoke in the chapter of the Jealous Man! First you say one thing and then another. The question of marriage is far removed from the purpose of Genius, whom we are discussing, for he never gave marriage a thought, the good man. Nor do you believe that he ever did, whatever you say, God help me. In your efforts to excuse Meun, you choose to read the passage as implying that one may licitly perform the said work, at least within marriage. Yet it seems inappropriate that in that state one should have to perform the work so fully and so diligently. Then, at the same time, he condemned the marriage state so excessively, when he said that there is so much strife in it that no one knowingly would enter into it, however eager to marry. How then, according to him, can the work of nature be continued? He ought rather to have praised the state of marriage, in which the work can licitly be performed, in order to whet man's appetite for marriage. But he does the very opposite. Therefore, it would seem that he did not intend it in the way that you suggest. And you yourself, in order to remedy the flaw, then say, on the question of whether marriage should be praised and to confirm that this was Meun's subject, that St. Augustine wrote: "The man who is not married thinks of divine things to please God, but the married man thinks of secular things to please his wife." Then you explain that you used this quotation for the benefit of those who seek to criticize the author unreasonably, although he is famous and had not been criticized previously. This is a masterly proof that Meun, in speaking so much of performing the work of nature, clearly intended it to be within the bonds of marriage! God! How well this is proved! Surely, this is like the common proverb about the glosses of Orleans which destroyed the text.

[106]

You still go on talking and launch into another long harangue, as always, to excuse your good master. But I do not plan to recount it all word for word. For it would annoy me too much, and does annoy me now, to speak at length on this subject. Besides, it is all to no purpose. You say that because everyone has not read the book of the *Rose,* you will quote the very words of Genius as they are in the book. Thus you quote, to be sure, many of his own words, but you pass over many others, choosing here and there those which most please you. Clearly, you have no desire to quote the evil that he says along with the good. You never forget that he says that one should make restitution to another and that one should be compassionate, merciful, and so on. True, and that one should do the works of God, in God's name, and then one will enter into paradise. But I believe that he wished to be a member of the order and the sect of rascals, and thus mingled venom with honey, and sweet liqueur with bile. Behold, the good it contains!

I do not know why we are debating these questions so fully, for I do not believe that we will be able to change each other's opinions. You say that he is good; I say that he is evil. Now show me which of the two is right. And when you and your accomplices, in your subtle ways, have been able to change evil into good, then will I believe that the *Roman de la Rose* is good. But I know well that this book is suitable for those who desire to live in wickedness and are more concerned with selfishly protecting themselves than others. For those, however, who desire to live in virtuous simplicity and not embroiled in worldly desires, deceiving none, nor being deceived, this book has little to offer. And indeed I would prefer to be among his opponents than among his accomplices, for I believe that the wolf has the smaller part. As the good man who composed the above-mentioned complaint said: "Would to God that such a rose had never been planted in the garden of Christianity." Nevertheless, you call yourself one of his disciples. And since you wish to be so, be so. For my part, I renounce his discipline. I embrace another which I believe is more worthwhile and which is more pleasing to me. And since I am far from being alone in this opinion, I do not understand why you his disciples single me out for attack. There is no honor at all in attacking the weakest opponent. There are numerous learned men, reliable and wise, as well as some great princes of this kingdom, and knights, and nobles, and many others who share my opinion, holding this book to be useless and dishonorable. Why do all of you together not attack the great trunk of the tree and strive to uproot it, destroying the root, from which the sap and juices flow, rather than attacking the little upper branches, which have no strength. In your misguided effort to destroy the tree utterly, you attack me, who am no stronger than the voice of a small cricket who all day beats his tiny wings and makes great noise, and is nothing in comparison with the high, delightful song of the gracious birds.

[107]

But you say that you cannot marvel enough how anybody dares to blame not only him but also those who prize and love his book of the *Rose*. My answer. I cannot marvel enough how anybody dare undertake to praise this book, which contains much that is likely to lead the human heart into damnable error. You say for your part that, rather than be numbered among such subtle critics, you prefer to be reproached for prizing and loving his book. In this, you remind me of the woman who said that she would prefer to be called *meretrix* by her lover than to be crowned queen.[7] Obviously, the most pleasing wishes are not always the most reasonable.

You say everybody should know that there remain yet seven thousand who are fully ready to defend him. My answer. It is a

---

[7] See *Roman de la Rose,* 8821-24.

general rule that an evil sect grows apace like a weed, but quantity
does not imply quality. And, God willing, there will not be such   [108]
a profusion of them henceforth. Meun's worth is not at all an
article of the faith; one may believe as he wishes. You say that if
he had been contemporary with those of us who blame him that
you would believe we have particular hatred for him personally.
But since we have never seen him, you cannot imagine from whence
this comes. My answer. Since we have never seen him, nor ever
been mistreated by him, you have the better reason for thinking
— since an enemy ought not to be believed — that true right, pure
truth moves us. If not from hatred, you say, it must come from
the loftiness of the book, which invites the winds of Envy. Ignorance, you say, is clearly not the cause of it all, nor is an inadequate
reading of the book. My answer. Since you concede that it was not
from ignorance, you may be sure that it was not envy which led
that good man to blame the book, for I am convinced that the
height of his elevated life precludes envy. Despite my own admitted ignorance, I assure you I feel no envy. And why should I?
He makes me neither hot nor cold, does me neither good nor
ill; he neither gives nor takes away; he does not speak of my particular situation — why then should I feel indignant? For I am
not married, nor hope to be, nor am I a nun, so that nothing he
says pertains to me. I am not Fair Welcome: I do not fear that
Old Woman; I do not have any rose buds to guard. Yet I assure
you that I love beautiful, wise, and well-written books. I seek them
out and read them eagerly (within the limits of my understanding),
and if I do not love that book of the *Rose,* it is simply because the
work teaches an evil and dishonorable lesson, and sows far more
evil than good. Moreover, the book, in my judgment, can be the
cause of eternal damnation as well as great harm in this life to
those who hear and delight in it; it inculcates dishonorable morals.
Thus I swear to you on my soul and by my faith that no other
cause moves me. You then surmise that we blame it in order to
stimulate people to read it, remarking that in such a case, our
opinion would be good: rest assured that this is certainly not
our intent.

After all this, you attribute to me greater worth than I actually   [109]
have, for which I thank you, and you beg me to guard the honor
that I have. And if, you go on, someone has praised me because

I have fired a shot over the towers of Notre Dame, I should not attempt to hit the moon with a cannon ball. Further, you warn me to avoid resembling the crow who, when its song was praised, began to sing louder and let the mouthful fall. My answer. Nothing gives one so much authority as one's own experience. Hence, in this case I can speak the truth from certain knowledge. You admonish, or rather accuse, me of self-pride. Yet I swear to you on my faith that I have never presumed to shoot as high as the towers of Notre Dame. How could I consider reaching higher or, thinking to sing louder, drop my morsel; for I do not consider my deeds or knowledge of any great worth. There is nothing more to be said, save that I can confess, in truth, that I love study and the solitary life so much that by cultivating them I may perhaps have gathered some lowly little flowers from the garden of delights, rather than climbing the tall trees to gather the beautiful, sweet-smelling, and tasty fruit — not, certainly, that the appetite and will are lacking, but that the weakness of my understanding prevents me, and even, I must confess, the fragrance of the little flowers, from which I have made slender garlands. Although I would never have dreamed of sending them out, those people who desired to have such garlands were amazed at my efforts, not, I recognize, for the greatness, but the novelty, of the thing. Although these my little flowers lay hidden for a long time, they are no longer so, although I assure you that they were not brought to light at my request. If you retort that some of my things were written on behalf of particular people, this has long since been common knowledge. I do not say this by way of excuse, for I need none. I merely seek to counter any possible opinion that I laid claim to any authority in my work. Therefore, I beg you and those who share your view not to bear a grudge against me on account of my previous work or of the present debate on the book of the *Rose*. For the debate began, as it were, accidentally and not deliberately, whatever my feeling. To confirm this, see my little work, in which I laid out completely the terms of our debate. It would disturb me greatly to be subject to such tyranny that I would not dare to speak the truth according to my conscience without its being turned against me. Rather, it should lead a wiser man than I to think more deeply than he has done for a long time, for as the proverb says, "Sometimes the fool can advise the wise man." Further, of no worth is your remark

[110]

that Holy Church, in which there have been so many worthy men
since the book was written, has let it pass for such a long time
without reproach, waiting on me and others to attack it. For you
know that each thing has its time, and, across the space of years,
nothing is long. It often happens that a great boil is cured by a
small needle point. How, for example, has Holy Church allowed
the opinion of the Conception of Our Lady, which is a far more
notable thing, to exist for so long a time, without reproaching
anyone for it. And, with regard to the Conception, there has hardly
ever been a topic so much and so widely debated amid such dissension, and yet it is not an article of the Faith, nor is this problem.
Every man, therefore, may believe what pleases him. For my part,
I do not intend to write any more about the matter, whoever may
write to me, for I have not undertaken to drink the entire Seine.
What I have written is written. I do not, I hasten to add, keep
quiet for fear of sending forth mistaken opinions, although my lack
of ingenuity and knowledge deprive me of an elegant style. I prefer
to devote myself to another subject more to my taste. Finally, I
ask all those who see my modest writing to remedy the defects of
my knowledge out of consideration for my person, and to take
everything in the pure spirit in which it was written. Otherwise,
I would prefer never to suggest anything. I will now bring to an
end my writing in this debate, which has never been spiteful, but
was begun, continued, and ended pleasantly, without personal en-
mity. Thus I pray the blessed Perfect Trinity and Supernal Wisdom
that you and all those who particularly love knowledge and the
nobility of good morals be illumined with such true light that you
may be admitted to celestial joy. Amen.

Written and completed by me Christine de Pisan, the second
day of October, 1402.

Your well wisher
Friend of knowledge
Christine   [111

XV

JEAN GERSON'S REPLY TO PIERRE COL

[This letter, written in Latin, is Jean Gerson's answer to Pierre Col's attack on Christine de Pisan and Lady Theological Eloquence. Believing it prior to Christine's reply, Potansky placed this some time before October, 1402. It seems clear from certain of Gerson's remarks that his reply to Col came after Christine's, and therefore we suggest a date some time after October 2, 1402. The text is in Ward, pp. 77-82.]

O Learned Man and most beloved Brother in the love of Christ, you have written things about me which I can in no way lay claim to. For I do not hold myself worthy of such honor. Rather, I am astonished at this praise which you have mingled with trivialities and indeed with (forgive me, brother, if I speak the truth) falsehood and folly. It happens, nonetheless, that despite my preoccupation, my zeal would not let me postpone answering you, being obliged as I am to return love for love and to satisfy you. I do not accuse you of feigning — for such is not your manner — but believe that you are simply showing your love for me. My response comes too from the belief that you have full confidence in that man whom you have praised so highly. For my very profession obliges me to strive against errors and vices as much as possible. Consequently, I recently published the fruits of a day's work, an allegorical oration in French, attacking not a Foolish Lover but rather written words and pictures which solicit, stimulate, and urge illicit love affairs more bitter than death. Yet I will not repeat nor turn into eloquent Latin those controversial matters which you have

already read in that work. For I believe that the peroration of that
work sufficiently condemns and casts out of the republic of the
Christian religion such words and pictures which provoke to lustful
licentiousness. This fact is understood by everyone who is enlight-   [77]
ened by the Catholic faith and in no way corrupted by vicious passion. Nevertheless, what kind of oration can hope to persuade those
who do not wish to be persuaded, who prefer their error, who are
blinded by the evil of those people who have given themselves over
to wicked thinking, who avert their eyes lest they see, and commit
that most grievous kind of wickedness so that they may delight in
their own evil ways and flatter themselves by lying about their
iniquities. Among such I am not obliged to number you, beloved
brother, and I humbly pray that I am never forced to do so.

I do intend, however, to pluck out some of those matters in
your writing of late yesterday which call for correction or deletion.
Why do I say *some,* when almost everything (I am speaking to
you as a brother) in one way or another cries out for censure?
Therefore, as soon as you regain possession of that writing, if I
am any judge, the greedy flame will consume it or, torn into tiny
pieces, it will remain in eternal oblivion. Above all, I wish to warn
you and those like you, lest such an exaggerated admiration of this
author, who should scarcely be numbered among even mediocre
writers, leads one to believe that you are ignorant of wiser authors,
who tower over him like a British whale over a dolphin or a cypress
over a shrub. Now, take heed of the pit which your attempt at
theology has opened before you. For example, you say that a boy
of two or three is in the State of Innocence. This is the Pelagian
heresy; [1] any man who holds it stubbornly must be considered an
heretic. Moreover, the many arguments that you advance to confound invincible reason bind you tighter and tighter in the knots
of that same heresy, like birds caught in lime, entangling themselves more and more by their efforts to escape. So harmful and
deadly is it to fight against the truth. Do not read just me, but
Augustine in *De Nuptiis & Concupiscentia,* especially in the second
book: you will see what I say. For you have believed, as I judge,
what you should not have believed, that a boy is in the state of

---

[1] The heresy of Pelagius, a monk of the 4th-5th century, who denied the
doctrine of Original Sin.

innocence, either because he is ignorant or because he is not yet guilty of committing sin. But you should have considered the original corruption of diseased concupiscence, which brings all men to ruin. I am amazed that you wrote what you did with no feeling of shame or regret. For example, you say that a Foolish Lover alone can judge rightly concerning such a wicked, nay even mad, passion. Consequently, you believe that a stranger to such passion (as you, not I, hold me to be) sees it only in a glass darkly, as if it behoove all those who would judge vices with the proper disinterest to be first corrupted by those same vices. Nothing could be further from the truth. Nobody judges wicked works more perversely than those who have been corrupted by the feverish sting or fatal sickness of such deeds, "who have become abominable in their desires." [2] Thus many evils arise from sensuality. No corrupt judge examines the truth well, as Horace said. [3] But when you add that the secret members of women were formerly sanctified by custom, I do not know what kind of Bible taught you, unless perhaps you had one in your possession different from ours. Or if not, that passage of Luke II.23 influences you and leads you astray: "Every male opening the womb shall be called holy to the Lord." What, I pray, "shall be called holy to the Lord"? If you say nothing, I answer: the first-born. Further, you say that your author, nay almost your god, wrote a great many good things, many of which are far above the general knowledge of all learned men and require, therefore, a ten-fold reading before they are understood. And what of it, since he mixed in a great many exceedingly evil things which contradict and outnumber those good ones? What remains to be said, save that he in the manner of a Foolish Lover was wild, changeable, quarrelsome, and, as Terence says, bent on "raging reasonably." [4] Therefore, that work is rigthly called a formless chaos, a Babylonian confusion, and a German broth, like Proteus changing into all his shapes. That familiar line sung to boys sums it up well:

The man who is at odds with himself is suitable for no one.

[78]

---

[2] Ps. XIII.1.
[3] *Satires*, II.ii.8-9.
[4] *Eunuchus*, 59.

Then concerning what you mentioned about theologians falling into foolish love at times, with which you indeed threatened me, may the true God of love, not false Cupid, preserve me from such a misfortune. That position of yours seemed to me more suited to the defamation of theologians than appropriate to the case in hand, as if by casting greater guilt upon theologians you and your cronies could thereby mitigate or conceal his crimes or even represent them as good. When Cicero described an eloquent man by saying that he is a good man skilled in speaking,[5] how much more when I speak of theologian, ought I to believe him to be a good man learned in sacred knowledge. Take heed too lest your author has spoken dishonorably out of prejudice. Explain who compelled him to introduce those things which Reason spoke in such an obscene and impure discourse. Further, your author deserves blame, not because he introduced Nature speaking of God, but because of the way in which she spoke of those mysteries which free and supernatural revelation alone can provide. In your attack on my little book, you placed me alongside a remarkable lady, to whom your work is ostensibly addressed, but so chaotically that you jump from her to Theological Eloquence and just as quickly back again. Yet since it was dedicated to her, I ask you if that heroine argued this erroneous thing set in a proverb: "It is better to deceive than to be deceived"? Did she not, rather, refute it and rightly so? The very anxiety and ingenuity of your evasiveness show that the [79] woman had you hard pressed with the sharpness of her reasoning. This is clear from your retreat to the position that the book had been disfigured in the disputed place by a spurious interpolation, since you do not say, nor do I see, how you could possibly have known this fact. Then this lady shrewdly pointed out that not only queens but also any right-minded person endowed with natural modesty would blush at a reading of your author, and that your own writings, whether you like it or not, show that you have the same sense of shame: for your naturally good disposition would not permit you to utter obscenity therein. It does not follow, as you would have it, that these people who show embarassment reveal

---

[5] Surely, Gerson intends Quintilian. See *Institutio Oratoria,* I, preface 9 and XII.i.1, where Quintilian cites Cato as his source: "Sit ergo nobis orator, quem constituimus, is, qui a M. Catone finitur, 'vir bonus dicendi peritus'."

their guilt on that account. Rather, it is a salutary thing if they blush, as Terence once said. [6]

I shall not touch on all matters; otherwise, I would have to comment on almost every line of yours. Yet when you assert that it is contrary to the natural appetite of mankind for one man to remain married to one woman, and vice versa, your statement is not only false but contradictory to your own previous declaration. When you were defending Genius the god of Nature, for example, you said that he spoke of the single wedding bond. Furthermore, what kind of attitude is this that you seek to hide the vileness of your author by teaching that he portrays evil so that it can be recognized and avoided. You cite, therefore, a certain love-captive of your acquaintance, who cured himself of his amorous sickness with this book of honeyed poison, and made his antidote out of its venom. Surely, all such thinking is nonsense. Your assertion that some men claim that the Song of Songs was composed in praise of the daughter of Pharoah is scarcely a Catholic view: for whoever said this lied against the Faith. But your argument that recourse must be made to the book is more invidious. The book, you say, does not contain all that the criticism of it implies. I do not want to resist any longer; I prefer to surrender and yield, rather than allow such a dishonest and dangerous reading to be repeated. Further, you remark at the end of your letter that those people who cheapened the book genuflected before Baal. I will say freely what I think: that interpretation of yours, if indeed it were serious, actually distorts the inner meaning and is vicious, and, being scandalous, injurious, false and smacking of heresy in Faith and morals, ought to be destroyed. Despite your great praise of me, you could never extol my virtue as much as you have condemned it by your unfounded suggestion — if indeed you were speaking seriously — that in reality I wrote my criticisms of the *Rose* in order to stir up a fiercer flame to burn men (whom we know to be eager for what is forbidden) [7] and to stimulate them to read this book again and again. This would be as if I should turn my profession into a lie, as if my duty should be to act falsely in doctrine and morals, and as

---

[6] *Adelphi,* 643.

[7] Cf. Ovid, Amores, III.iv.17: "nitimur in vetitum semper cupimusque negata."

if I myself, like your author, should speak the opposite of my true intent, yea even to set myself at odds with the Christian faith. May I die before I am ever considered a defender of this work. Ask yourself rather whether deception of this kind has not polluted your own author: for while at times he condemns carnal love, he more [80] frequently praises it, and why not, acording to your conception, since he can thereby render easily-swayed spirits more prone to love. What can I say about that protestation of your author which he tried to draw over himself like a cloak for his filth? "I have," he says, "put in nothing that was mine alone." [8] He therefore asserts that he merely quotes these things and did not originate them. Wherefore, you, his admirers, do not seek to praise him if he spoke well, since he himself, in bringing controversial matters into the book, denies responsibility for wicked words which might bring shame on it. Do not, therefore, grow so hot with passion in hatred against us, and do not declaim against us with such bombastic words and swelled-out cheeks, if this book is guilty in its own right. For we censure not characters but writings (whoever made them), since one who gives a poisoned drink, even if it is mixed by someone else, must not be judged free of guilt on that account. Great God, this is just like a man testifying, and at the same time contradicting his own testimony. Such a tactic is no excuse for him; rather he acts like the man of whom it is said: "out of your own mouth I judge you, wicked servant." [9]

But, finally, I have never injured you, O Christian Court, neither in spirit nor in word. You cannot, I confess, correct all evils. Otherwise, what should be preserved for divine justice in the future? In many cases, condemnation is provided through edicts and ordinary laws, as against simony, theft, homicide, adultery; so it is with this most contagious license of evil speaking and writing, especially where no official prosecutor steps forward. In no way, however, do I propose to excuse many men of the ecclesiastic estate for having preserved, to the destruction of many men, not only the many books of Ovid but also occult writings, and especially the book now under discussion.

---

[8] Cf. *Roman de la Rose,* 15135-302, where Meun apologizes for the work.
[9] Luke XIX.22.

I excuse those who were not officially required to censure, and yet who spontaneously in speech or writing, generally or specifically, condemned such things, as I do now and as many did before. Thus I approve that which is written in the Acts of the Apostles, XIX.19: "All those newly converted to the faith, who were followers of curious arts, burned their books to the value of fifty thousand pieces of silver." Behold, before God, I do not lie. And if you have ever had any confidence in me, believe me when I say that if the only copy of your author's book, worth a thousand pounds and more, belonged to me, I would cast it into the flames to be consumed, rather than sell it to be published. See how deeply I am moved, not indeed to read it again and not certainly out of ignorance as you allege (although I am greatly ignorant) but for the sake of my conscience and the conscience of others. Remember, therefore, I first drank long ago in my youth at all, or almost all, those foun-tains from which the writings of your author have poured forth [81] translated, like little streams: such as Boethius, Ovid, Terence, Juvenal, Alanus de Insulis, Guillaume de Saint-Amour, Abelard and Heloise, Martianus Capella, and many others. Be assured that for the depth of its knowledge I would not hesitate to match Master Bonaventure's small book *The Journey of the Mind to God,* which I read in a day, with your entire book, yes even with ten like it. Yet you believe us to be too brutish and too dense to be able to understand this book of yours. Further, to your advice that I read it again to understand it, I answer: Read, brother, and read again the fourth book of *De Doctrina Christiana,* for that work poses a great many more problems than your book in French. Augustine will make it clear to you, believe me, that I did no great injury in associating Eloquence with Theology. He will make you feel ashamed, perhaps, for your audacity in asserting what you have not fully understood. Augustine plainly contradicts you, now with the most express words in that same fourth book of *De Doctrina Chris-tiana,* now in the very opening of the work by his style and great powers of eloquence. Nevertheless, I spoke very temperately, if you had but noticed, when I introduced Theological Eloquence speaking in the moderate form of discourse, [10] for I carefully avoided that preciousness about which you are challenging me. Finally, most

---

[10] See Augustine, *De Doctrina Christiana,* IV.

excellent man and most worthy for the protection of a better cause, let us be serious; let the desire to win or merely to chatter be silenced: let us come to the serious, religious matter. I affirm to you that if I knew that my own brother had composed and published such a book, and, having been sufficiently warned and condemned, still persisted in his error, then, if he had died impenitent, I would no more pray to our Lord Jesus Christ for him than for the damned. With this, farewell, and may you devote yourself henceforth to healthier and purer studies, so that you may not give occasion of scandal to the common people. And if some harsh words of mine have perhaps offended you, forgive me for assuming that you shared my view, for I did it out of affection. Finally, regard the whole matter as stemming from the zeal for Catholic truth and an earnest desire for your salvation. And let us pray for one another that we may be saved.   [82]

XVI

JEAN DE MONTREUIL
UT SUNT MORES

[This Latin letter was probably written between the beginning of October and the beginning of December, 1402. Laurent de Premierfait, according to Potansky, may have been the recipient. The Latin text is in Ornato, I, 220-221, Letter 154.]

Concerning the varying customs and conditions of men, I will make unpleasant disclosures. O famous man, you will see and hear, in one of my writings in the vernacular, how unfairly, unjustly, and arrogantly some people have accused and attacked the most excellent Master Jean de Meun. I speak especially of a certain woman named Christine, who has just recently published her writings, and who, within feminine limitations, is not, admittedly, lacking in intelligence, but who, nevertheless, sounds to me like "Leontium the Greek whore," as Cicero says, "who dared to criticize the great philosopher Theophrastus." [1] These harsh critics assert that that same most ingenious man erred in many passages of his very famous work of the *Rose* and spoke immoderately as a wanton man: first of all, in the chapter of Reason, his invented character Reason spoke, as they say, dishonorably; next, the Jealous Man expressed himself without restraint; and, finally, Meun himself in the conclusion of his work through the character of the Lover voiced his youthful passions indecently, excessively, and, as they add, lubri-

---

[1] Cicero, *De natura deorum*, I.93.

ciously. "O times, O customs![2] I am almost beside myself," as
Terence says.[3] O that such a work, that such a man, whom our
age has not equalled, nor, I predict, will the future, should be torn
in this way by the nails of detraction, by headstrong word-mongers
criticizing a dead man, by those whom he could overwhelm, were
he alive, with a single nod. These detractors, clearly, have no under-   [220]
standing of the variety of his characters and do not perceive by
what emotions and passions they are driven, nor to what end or
purpose they were made to speak. And, finally, they simply do not
understand how that teacher has fulfilled the function of a satirist
and is therefore permitted many things which are prohibited to
other writers.

I would get angry and protest against those slanderers if I had
not learned from the ancients how many very excellent men of the
military and scholarly profession everywhere have always gladly
accepted the stain of such a sacrifice. For it is not true that high
genius escapes such barking dogs or the bites of enviers, as the
prophet and king testifies: it is not possible to "stop the mouths
of those who speak evil,"[4] Just as in Livy's aphorism, "the greater
the glory, the greater the envy."[5]

But what is so very irritating to me is that there exist, among
the people who criticize us so severely, some who as they themselves admit have only read the work incompletely; and although
some others may have studied it, they are by no means, believe
me, capable of understanding so high a conception or of attaining
to its mystery — a book that could better be called a mirror or a
discourse of human life than a romance. And granted that the book
was more attentively read by one of these detractors and, that
brooding over the processes and the nuances of the work, it was
given to him to understand, still he was led to speak and feel differently because of his religious vocation and his vows, or perhaps
he is simply the kind of man who is rendered useless for the prop-
agation of the species, which is, after all, the purpose of this book.
But who does not condemn the judgment of such detractors? Who

---

[2] Ornato cites Cicero, *Verr.,* IV.56; *In Catil.,* I.2; *Pro domo sua,* 137;
Pro Deiot., 31.

[3] *Andria,* 937.

[4] Ps. LXII.12.

[5] *Ab urbe condita,* XXXV.x.5.

indeed, as Petrarch said, do not know, or else neglect, what they castigate in others. [6]

Concerning this matter, dear brother, you should, I think, keep your skills in readiness, because of your regard for that extraordinary philosopher and poet, whom you rightly venerate, love, and honor. For you surpass all others of this kingdom in the style of Meun himself. Therefore, may your sublime muse inspire you to declaim strongly against these slanderers, defending with your staff this highest teacher of morals, so that they may know, if indeed the mind can be stirred by arguments, what it is to speak against a man bolstered and honored by such knowledgeable and powerful disciples and friends.

Farewell, and humbly recommend me to my teacher and master John Venator, and forgive me that I have boldly addressed you in the familiar form, "tu." For I have learned from a reading of the ancients that a single person should not be addressed by the plural number.

[221]

---

[6] Ornato reports that he has been unable to locate this quotation, a dilemma we share.

XVII

JEAN DE MONTREUIL
EX QUO NUGE

*[In this letter, Montreuil appears to be humbly seeking approval
of his part in the debate from a highly admired superior, while
apparently smarting from an earlier and unexpected criticism by
him. The recipient was likely Pierre d'Ailly. It was written in
late 1402, between the beginning of November and the beginning of December. The Latin text is in Ornato, I, 218-219,
Letter 152.]*

Since our light French verses are not worthy for your eyes, O
reverend father, I have decided to write in Latin prose. I am,
therefore, my learned master, enclosing two letters recently composed
with no less enthusiasm than those petty works in a different genre:
the one commending that famous work of the *Rose*; the other, in
the form of a satire on the same subject, attacking that man who   [218]
attacked you satirically, albeit on other grounds. I most humbly
beseech you not to consider them too insignificant to merit your time
and attention. But I take heart that these humble efforts may be
invigorated by passing through your house of wisdom, and not
returned, like my *Proverbs,* as works beneath contempt. "Socrates,"
the most learned of all men, according to the oracle of Appollo, [1]
"did not blush to play with boys. Scipio Affricanus and Cato the
Censor, those great men, delighted in counting pebbles in the sand." [2]

---

[1] Cicero, *Academica,* I.16; *de Senectute,* XXI.78; *de Amicitia,* II.7.
[2] Seneca, *de Tranquillitate animi,* XVII.4; Cicero, *de Oratore,* II.vi.23.

But you will scorn absolutely the schoolboy's rule and compass, and the man you ought to stimulate to study by your charm you will cause to despair of success. Yet let such conduct be no part of your humanity, nor of your paternal affection and outstanding benevolence! Let it be rather the custom of the barbarians, not your own. Up to the present time, you have behaved in this way toward no one, as far as I have heard. And will John be the first to be struck with this rod? the first to be subjected to this misfortune? And I who was confident of having a protector and friend, shall I have a mordant critic? May I not expect, even if Cicero taught otherwise, and even strongly assert that I may rather anticipate the applause and guidance of a truer kindness from the innate goodness of your love? May you look upon me with a benevolent eye, so that I will not be driven to seek another refuge, but let the Provost of Lisle [3] obtain that indulgence which he has always prayed for with pious supplications. "And if there is anything sinful, we will correct it with you as judge," as Terence advises. [4] Farewell.　　　　　[219]

---

[3] i.e., Montreuil himself. Montreuil's words are *prepositus Insule*; he is obviously punning on his own office as Provost of Lille.

[4] *Hecyra,* 253-255.

XVIII

JEAN GERSON
POENITEMINI: PAR LE MERVEILLEUX

[*This sermon was preached by Gerson on the seventeenth day of December, 1402, in the Church of St. Jean-en-Grève. The text of the sermon may be consulted in Jean Gerson, Œuvres complètes, ed. Mgr. Glorieux (Paris: Desclée & Cie, 1968), VII, 822-832.*]

… …

Reading books which stimulate lust is particularly dangerous, lest it be a mortal sin. And men who own such books should be required by their confessors to burn them or tear them up, so that neither they nor anyone else might sin any longer in that way — books like Ovid's, or, say, Matheolus',[1] or parts of the *Roman de la Rose,* or rondeaux and ballades, or excessively dissolute songs. Judge then what penance must be done by those who write and publish such books, a subject which I have already written fully about. I say the same about filthy and dishonorable paintings.

[829

… …

Should a man who has led someone astray by his deed or his words be responsible for bringing him back to the right path? I answer, "Yes, with all his might." Indeed, it must be imposed on him as a penance; that is what I do with everyone. Note[2] how

---

[1] The *Lamentations,* a famous thirteenth-century anti-feminist satirical work.

[2] Here and elsewhere in his sermons, Gerson seems simply to be reminding himself of points that he wishes to make.

the *Roman de la Rose* speaks against this, wherein the character Reason herself speaks bawdily, using inflammatory words which encite men to lechery. This is why such words are to be forbidden. Take note of Seneca: "Shameful things," etc.; Aristotle, Book V of the *Politics*; Noah and Ham; Cicero; and St. Augustine. Take note of the peril of the *Roman de la Rose* and similar things, etc.; and of the filthiness of the end [i.e., of the *Roman de la Rose*], etc., *videatur finis*. Take note of the child who remembers the evil in the Romance. Note that he [Jean de Meun] is damned if he did not repent. Note that his efforts increase the sufferings which befall him. [3]

[831]

... ...

---

[3] This is quite enigmatic in its sparse form here, but elsewhere Gerson makes it clear that the continuing influence of the *Roman de la Rose* causes its author, if in hell or purgatory, increased punishment. See pages 49 and 165.

XIX

PIERRE COL'S ANSWER TO CHRISTINE DE PISAN
[FRAGMENT]

[This fragment of a letter is in answer to Christine de Pisan's defense of her position in her long reply to Pierre Col's first letter. If this extremely brief portion of a letter can serve as any indication, Pierre Col seems to be far more on the defensive at this point. The light bemused tone of the first letter seems to be missing. The letter was probably written some time in December, 1402. The Old French text is in Ward, pp. 112-113.]

To the woman of high understanding, Damoiselle Christine de Pisan

Since you are wise enough to realize that it is human to sin but that persistence in sin is the work of the devil, you have proposed to write no more harsh criticism of the *Roman de la Rose*; nevertheless you will not thereby keep me from restraining your excesses. For since you have written so many repetitious criticisms of so notable a writer, reason, by both justice and good custom, gives me the right to reply. As a disciple of Meun, I have responded only once up to this time, although, granted, there was scarcely a need of it, because even to my limited understanding a single reading of your evasions is answer enough. You have not obscured or blackened at all the truth that I uphold, nor do your extravagant explanations and elaborate language leave any stain on the lofty reputation of Master Jean de Meun. And I believe that it is for this exact reason that the Provost of Lisle has not answered you.

I myself was for some little while inclined not to answer you at all because of this fact, as well as for the fact that I have much else to concern myself with. Nevertheless, by disputing many points in order to learn and to exercise my skills I will respond to some particular facts and evasions put into your letter in answer to mine of the 30th day of October, and I ask that you hold as repeated my justification put into my other letter.

What you say a little before the end of your letter may indeed be true, that there is no honor at all in hanging a fool, that is, in attacking you who are the weakest part. Seeing that there are many wise teachers, great princes of the realm, and knights who are of your opinion, one ought rather, you say, to break down the great trunk and not concern himself with the small branches. And yet I have known no person who blamed him before or after you, save only he who composed the Complaint of Lady Eloquence. Yet you reproach me for having dared to criticize a work of so famous a clerk, which seems contradictory, and (may it not displease you) here and elsewhere you fall into the ditch that you had dug for me. This is clear enough evidence of such contradictions when you [112] say that we should direct our attacks at the more powerful ones and then criticize me for having done just that. When I think of that small branch I am reminded of the common proverb which runs: If he blames you, you do not need a great praise. O God glorious! How many people there are who have never craved fame for themselves, or who blame themselves somewhat in order to glorify themselves! This is why you call yourself a small branch, and nevertheless . . . [113]

XX

JEAN GERSON
POENITEMINI: EN BENOISTE JOURNEE

*[Gerson preached this sermon in St. Jean-en-Grève on December
24, 1402. At this time he speaks at length about the* Roman de
la Rose. *For the text, Glorieux, VII, 833-841.]*

... ...

The *Roman de la Rose* says that the sin by which a woman's body
is sullied is the least of sins. This! the cause of her abandoning
herself to all the other evils! Beware of those who steer women
into error in order to abuse them and make heretics of them.
Repent! Hasten to repent while there is time. Grasp that which
is certain. Repent!

[837]

... ...

Mouth [1] asks if naming the shameful members specifically and
speaking of such sinfulness is an unreasonable thing? And she
argues that it is not: first, on the authority of the *Roman de la
Rose*; secondly, by the reasons given therein. For of themselves
words are not at all shameful, and if the things are shameful, it is
because of sin. And there is sin too in murder and theft, about
which everybody speaks. To this Reason answers that calling the
shameful members by name may be done first of all (1) for de-

---

[1] Gerson's method in this sermon is to present general and common views
through those good *escoliers,* "students" — Heart, Eye, Ear, Nose, Mouth, and
Touch — and then to have Reason, clearly the voice of Gerson himself, sift
out and strongly oppose any error in such opinions.

bauchery, or (2) for enflaming oneself to lechery; further, it may be done (3) by means of a fictional character, or (4) for the purpose of good teaching or (5) among those who seek only the truth. [838] The first must not be done, and to say the contrary is error, like saying that people should walk about nude or that Ham should be excused for not covering his father. This is the error of those philosophers who, for this reason, were called dogs. This is what Aristotle forbade in the seventh book of the *Politics*. Seneca said: "you should not speak shameful things." Evil speaking leads to evil doing. St. Augustine says that it is an error to demean oneself. Cicero in *De officiis*: such language is called dirty and filthy. St. Paul says that many things done in private should not even be named; "corrupt good manners," [2] etc. I would wish that those who say the contrary would themselves teach their daughters to speak in that manner according to that Reason.

The second kind of conduct cannot be excused: even between married people decency must be preserved. The third ought not to be done publicly, for the reasons I have already given, as well as for the fact that truth and honor must be preserved in fictional characters. The fourth is permissible, and the fifth is in certain circumstances: a sick man, for example, will bare his body to a doctor in order to be cured. And if this is what Master Jean de Meun intended, he was right: but he was wrong (1) to make Reason speak in the manner of a Foolish Lover, (2) to exhort women and others to speak in a vulgar way, (3) to address his book to young people who misused it, (4) to show, by his arguments, that people ought to walk about nude. So I say in reply that the words are shameful because of the resulting evil, which is deliberately intended, as is looking at naked women because of the wicked desire which it stimulates. Take note of St. Augustine, *De nuptiis et concupiscentia,* and also the common proverb: he does no evil who intends none. Good people, take these books away from your daughters and children, because they will take the evil and leave the good. The example of the child, etc. [3] Note what is the purpose. Note the odes of Ovid, who was exiled because of them. Note Matheolus the fool.

---

[2] I Cor. XV.33.

[3] Apparently, simply Gerson's personal reminder of an *exemplum* he planned to use at this point in the sermon.

I make three assertions: (1) that if I had the only copy of the *Roman de la Rose,* worth a thousand pounds, I would burn it before I would sell it to be published in its present form. (2) If I knew that he had not repented of it, I would no more pray for him than for Judas. And those who read with evil intent increase his suffering if he is damned or in purgatory. (3) If I heard the confession of someone who misused the book, I would order him to destroy many things in it or to throw the whole thing out, and the same with dirty and inflammatory paintings, made for foolish lovers of both sexes.   [839]

... ...

XXI

JEAN DE MONTREUIL
SCIS ME

*[This letter seems to be addressed to Gontier Col, and was prob-
ably written at the end of December, 1402. The Latin text is
in Ornato, I, 179-181, Letter 120.]*

Most learned master and brother,[1] you know that, thanks to
your continual urging and encouragement, I have read that noble
work of Master Jean de Meun, commonly called the *Roman de la
Rose*. And because I stand with you in admiration of his art,
ability, and learning — and I assert irrevocably that I will persevere
in this belief — I am badly treated and censured most bitterly by
school men of no little authority, more than you would believe, so
that if I strive to defend him further, they clearly wish, as they
say, to proclaim me a heretic. And it is pointless to pretend that
you and many other worthy and learned men have shown the book
to be of such worth that they ought to honor it so much that
they would rather do without their shirt than this book and, in
no way, to prefer Meun's rivals to men of our own opinion. Indeed,
these rivals were so powerful that if there were anything reprehensible in the work, they would never have allowed it to survive
a single hour.[2] Neither does it help to beseech them to examine

---

[1] This letter was probably addressed to Gontier Col. Compare the first
sentence with a similar remark about Gontier in Document III of this work.

[2] This complex and tortuous sentence is practically impossible to translate.
The Latin text reads as follows: "Nec pretendere prodest te totque viros alios
valentes scientificos et perdoctos illum tanti fecisse pene ut colerent, utque

and appreciate, as simple justice requires, the basic nature of the
work — the grounds and occasions for his saying certain things and
making use of introduced characters — before they condemn so
great an author. Immediately they break in and interrupt my
words, so that I scarcely dare to move my lips, lest they threaten
me with the disgrace of anathema and firmly judge me worthy of
death.

What do you want me to say? What so greatly irritates me is
that they attack our master with insults, saying that he merits the
fire far more than a reading, and deem themselves to be contaminated by inexpiable sin if they should hear any part of him. In
the name of human justice I humbly beseech them not to condemn   [179]
him before they have thoroughly studied him, for I have made it
clear that the right of self-defense is given even to sacrilegious men,
traitors, and poisoners, and that it is not permissible to prejudge
anyone before examining his case. Yet we can do nothing, most
honored brother, but beat the air uselessly, passing the time. So
great is the obstinacy of man that we cannot hope to obtain anything. This is the temper of the time; this, the madness. For they
fear lest, conquered by us, they are obliged to yield by lamenting
Truth herself. Therefore, they clamor, as Lactantius said, and interrupt lest they hear; they close their eyes lest they see the light
which we offer, [3] observing the custom of the Jews against our
Saviour, according to which enemies are made judges. [4]

In this way our most deserving teacher is condemned, for all
his innocence, without a hearing, a procedure which all laws forbid,
by those who would not have attempted to even mutter in his

---

quam eo carere mallent camisia et nichilominus nostris correctoribus antepo-
nere suos emulos, qui, si quid reprehensionis inesset, adeo magni erant, ut
librum suum vivere nequaquam permisissent una hora." The problems involved
are, first of all, the precise meaning of *emulos* (Does it mean "enviers,"
"enemies," or simply "imitators"?); secondly, *correctoribus* (Does it mean
"correctors" in a hostile or friendly sense, or should it be rendered in our
admittedly rather bland phrase "men of our own opinion," which is suggested
more by general context than rigid definition?); and, finally, the ambiguity
of *suos, suum,* wherein the second use modifying book (the *Roman de la
Rose?*) suggests that it does not have its usual reflexive sense.

[3] This entire passage beginning with "they attack" is a very close, though
not exact, rendering of Lactantius' defense of his own work in *Divinae insti-
tutiones,* V.i.1.

[4] Deuteronomy, XXXII.31.

living presence. Yet they despise, execrate, and impugn him igno-
miniously, and, what is more annoying, do so without having
thoroughly read and studied the book. O the arrogance, temerity,
audacity! They even admit that they have read only superficially
and never thoroughly or completely, and yet they censure such a
work which was created and published with the sweat and toil of
so many days and nights. They are like those who having drunk
far too freely accuse and reproach and condemn as it pleases and
as the whimsical inspiration strikes. They judge so great a work as
of little more worth than the frivolous song of a jongleur written
in a day.

With regard to their false position, I attacked one of their
supporters, as you will see by the letter which this messenger brings
to you. Now, your duty as leader, prince, and guide of this enter-
prise will be to defend your most praiseworthy and most beloved
disciple [5] and to trample underfoot these feeble-minded and mad
ones, as well as to strengthen, sustain, and anoint my weak and
ill-organized reasons with the greater skill of your eloquence, since
I entered this field of battle, as I would not otherwise have done,
because I relied on your assistance and the power of your mind.
For I know that when the latent power of your mind is evoked
and the mute pen speaks forth, these enemies of truth shall not
prevail against us. [6] I am sure that when you choose, you can make
them like meek sheep and silent stumps. Farewell, and, as far as
you are able, do not allow your friends to be destroyed so unjustly,
cunningly, perniciously, and hostilely.

[180]

---

[5] The word is *imitatorem*. Compare footnote 4 to Document IV., p. 43.
[6] Ornato cites Ps. XII.5, but cf. Matthew XVI.18.

XXII

JEAN GERSON
POENITEMINI: BIEN A POINT ET APPROPOS

*[Again in St. Jean-en-Grève, Gerson preached this sermon, with
its brief and final reference to the* Roman de la Rose, *on December 31, 1402. The text may be consulted in Glorieux, VII,
851-856.]*

... ...

My good people, as I was thinking on this subject the other
day, I felt a debate arise in the depths of my heart on the question
of which form of chastity is the most commendable: whether virginity, marriage, or widowhood? But above all, I assumed that each
of these ladies was good and praiseworthy, for I know that some
heretics have wished to condemn the state of virginity; others, the
married state; others saw no worth in any chastity whatsoever, but
praised lechery, saying that it followed nature. And this is what
the *Roman de la Rose* says through its character Genius, the so-
called god of nature, and afterward the author in his own person
says the same thing even more disgustingly in the end of the work.   [852]

... ...

BIBLIOGRAPHY

Abensour, L. *La Femme et le féminisme avant la Révolution.* Paris: E. Leroux, 1923.

Beck, F. *Les Epistres sur le Roman de la Rose von Christine de Pizan nach drei Pariser Hss. bearbeitet und zum ersten Mal veroffentlicht.* Neuberg, 1888.

Christine de Pisan. *Œuvres Poétiques.* Ed. Maurice Roy. 3 vols. SATF 24. 1886; rpt. New York: Johnson Reprint Corporation, 1965.

Connolly, James L. *John Gerson, Reformer and Mystic.* Louvain: Uystpruyst, 1928.

Coville, A. *Gontier et Pierre Col et L'Humanisme en France au Temps de Charles VI.* Paris: Librairie E. Droz, 1934.

Dow, Blanche Hinman. *The Varying Attitude toward Women in French Literature of the Fifteenth Century: The Opening Years.* New York: Publications of the Institute of French Studies, Inc., 1936.

Du Castel, Françoise. *Damoiselle Christine de Pizan: Veuve de Me Etienne de Castel, 1364-1431.* Paris: Editions A. et J. Picard, 1972.

Fleming, John V. "The Moral Reputation of the Roman de la Rose before 1400," *Romance Philology,* 18 (1965), 430-435.

Fleming, John V. *The Roman de la Rose: A Study in Allegory and Iconography.* Princeton: Princeton University Press, 1969.

———. "Hoccleve's 'Letter of Cupid' and the 'Quarrel' over the Roman de la Rose," *Medium Aevum,* 40 (1971), 21-40.

Gerson, Jean. *Œuvres complètes.* Ed. Msr. Glorieux. Paris: Desclée & Cie, 1960-   .

———. *Six Sermons inédits.* Ed. Louis Mourin. Paris: J. Vrin, 1946.

Huizinga, Johan. *The Waning of the Middle Ages.* London: Edward Arnold & Company, 1937.

Kelly, F. Douglas. "Reflections on the Role of Christine de Pisan as a Feminist Writer," *Sub-Stance,* 2 (1972), 63-71.

Kilgour, Raymond. *The Decline of Chivalry as Shown in the French Literature of the Late Middle Ages.* Gloucester, Mass.: Peter Smith, 1966.

Langlois, Ernest. "Le Traité de Gerson contre Le Roman de la Rose," *Romania,* 45 (1919), 23-48.

Lorris, Guillaume and Jean de Meun. *Le Roman de la Rose.* Ed. Ernest Langlois. 5 vols. SATF 63. 1914; rpt. New York: Johnson Reprint Corporation, 1965.

Minto, W. "A Champion of her Sex," *MacMillan's Magazine,* 53 (1886), 264-275.

Montreuil, Jean de. *Opera.* Ed. Ezio Ornato. Vol. I: *Epistolario.* Torino: G. Giappichelli, 1963.

Piaget, A. "Chronologie des Epistres sur le Roman de la Rose." In *Etudes Romanes dédiées à Gaston Paris.* Paris: Bouillon, 1891.

Potansky, Peter. *Der Streit um den Rosenroman.* Munich: Wilhelm Fink Verlag, 1972.

Richardson, Lula McDowell. *The Forerunners of Feminism in French Literature of the Renaissance from Christine of Pisa to Marie de Gournay.* Diss. Johns Hopkins, 1929. Baltimore: Johns Hopkins University Press, 1929.

Rigaud, Rose. *Les Idées féministes de Christine de Pisan.* Thesis Neuchatel. Neuchatel: Imprimerie Attinger Frères, 1911.

Robertson, D. W., Jr. *A Preface to Chaucer. Studies in Medieval Perspectives.* Princeton: Princeton University Press, 1962.

Thomas, Antonius. *Joannis de Monsterolio: Vita et Operibus.* Paris, 1883.

Tuve, Rosamond. *Allegorical Imagery: Some Mediaeval Books and their Posterity.* Princeton: Princeton University Press, 1966.

Ward, Charles Frederick. *The Epistles on the Romance of the Rose and Other Documents in the Debate.* Diss. Chicago, 1911. Chicago, 1911.

NORTH CAROLINA STUDIES IN THE ROMANCE LANGUAGES AND LITERATURES

I.S.B.N. Prefix 0-8078-

Recent Titles

THE DRAMATIC WORKS OF ÁLVARO CUBILLO DE ARAGÓN, by Shirley B. Whitaker. 1975. (No. 149). *-949-9*.

A CONCORDANCE TO THE "ROMAN DE LA ROSE" OF GUILLAUME DE LORRIS, by Joseph R. Danos. 1976. (No. 156). *0-88438-403-9*.

POETRY AND ANTIPOETRY: A STUDY OF SELECTED ASPECTS OF MAX JACOB'S POETIC STYLE, by Annette Thau. 1976. (No. 158). *-005-X*.

FRANCIS PETRARCH, SIX CENTURIES LATER, by Aldo Scaglione. 1975. (No. 159).

STYLE AND STRUCTURE IN GRACIÁN'S "EL CRITICÓN", by Marcia L. Welles. 1976. (No. 160). *-007-6*.

MOLIERE: TRADITIONS IN CRITICISM, by Laurence Romero. 1974 (Essays, No. 1). *-001-7*.

CHRÉTIEN'S JEWISH GRAIL. A NEW INVESTIGATION OF THE IMAGERY AND SIGNIFICANCE OF CHRÉTIEN DE TROYES'S GRAIL EPISODE BASED UPON MEDIEVAL HEBRAIC SOURCES, by Eugene J. Weinraub. 1976. (Essays, No. 2). *-002-5*.

STUDIES IN TIRSO, I, by Ruth Lee Kennedy. 1974. (Essays, No. 3). *-003-3*.

VOLTAIRE AND THE FRENCH ACADEMY, by Karlis Racevskis. 1975. (Essays, No. 4). *-004-1*.

THE NOVELS OF MME RICCOBONI, by Joan Hinde Stewart. 1976. (Essays, No. 8). *-008-4*.

FIRE AND ICE: THE POETRY OF XAVIER VILLAURRUTIA, by Merlin H. Forster. 1976. (Essays, No. 11). *-011-4*.

THE THEATER OF ARTHUR ADAMOV, by John J. McCann. 1975. (Essays, No. 13). *-013-0*.

AN ANATOMY OF POESIS: THE PROSE POEMS OF STÉPHANE MALLARMÉ, by Ursula Franklin. 1976. (Essays, No. 16). *-016-5*.

LAS MEMORIAS DE GONZALO FERNÁNDEZ DE OVIEDO, Vols. I and II, by Juan Bautista Avalle-Arce. 1974. (Texts, Textual Studies, and Translations, Nos. 1 and 2). *-401-2; 402-0*.

GIACOMO LEOPARDI: THE WAR OF THE MICE AND THE CRABS, translated, introduced and annotated by Ernesto G. Caserta. 1976. (Texts, Textual Studies. and Translations, No. 4). *-404-7*.

LUIS VÉLEZ DE GUEVARA: A CRITICAL BIBLIOGRAPHY, by Mary G. Hauer. 1975. (Texts, Textual Studies, and Translations, No. 5). *-405-5*.

UN TRÍPTICO DEL PERÚ VIRREINAL: "EL VIRREY AMAT, EL MARQUÉS DE SOTO FLORIDO Y LA PERRICHOLI". EL "DRAMA DE DOS PALANGANAS" Y SU CIRCUNSTANCIA. estudio preliminar, reedición y notas por Guillermo Lohmann Villena. 1976. (Texts, Textual Studies, and Translation, No. 15). *-415-2*.

LOS NARRADORES HISPANOAMERICANOS DE HOY, edited by Juan Bautista Avalle-Arce. 1973. (Symposia, No. 1). *-951-0*.

ESTUDIOS DE LITERATURA HISPANOAMERICANA EN HONOR A JOSÉ J. ARROM, edited by Andrew P. Debicki and Enrique Pupo-Walker. 1975. (Symposia, No. 2). *-952-9*.

MEDIEVAL MANUSCRIPTS AND TEXTUAL CRITICISM, edited by Christopher Kleinhenz. 1976. (Symposia, No. 4). *-954-5*.

SAMUEL BECKETT. THE ART OF RHETORIC. edited by Edouard Morot-Sir, Howard Harper, and Dougald McMillan III. 1976. (Symposia, No. 5). *-955-3*.

DELIE. CONCORDANCE, by Jerry Nash. 1976. 2 Volumes. (No. 174).

FIGURES OF REPETITION IN THE OLD PROVENÇAL LYRIC: A STUDY IN THE STYLE OF THE TROUBADOURS, by Nathaniel B. Smith. 1976. (No. 176). *-9176-2*.

When ordering please cite the *ISBN Prefix* plus the last four digits for each title.

Send orders to: University of North Carolina Press
North Carolina 27514
Chapel Hill
U. S. A.

NORTH CAROLINA STUDIES IN THE
ROMANCE LANGUAGES AND LITERATURES

I.S.B.N. Prefix 0-8078-

Recent Titles

A CRITICAL EDITION OF LE REGIME TRESUTILE ET TRESPROUFITABLE POUR CON-SERVER ET GARDER LA SANTE DU CORPS HUMAIN, by Patricia Willett Cummins. 1977. (No. 177).

THE DRAMA OF SELF IN GUILLAUME APOLLINAIRE'S "ALCOOLS", by Richard Howard Stamelman. 1976. (No. 178). -9178-9.

A CRITICAL EDITION OF "LA PASSION NOSTRE SEIGNEUR" FROM MANUSCRIPT 1131 FROM THE BIBLIOTHEQUE SAINTE-GENEVIEVE, PARIS, by Edward J. Gallagher. 1976. (No. 179). -9179-7.

A QUANTITATIVE AND COMPARATIVE STUDY OF THE VOCALISM OF THE LATIN INSCRIPTIONS OF NORTH AFRICA, BRITAIN, DALMATIA, AND THE BALKANS, by Stephen William Omeltchenko. 1977. (No. 180). -9180-0.

OCTAVIEN DE SAINT-GELAIS "LE SEJOUR D'HONNEUR", edited by Joseph A. James. 1977. (No. 181). -9181-9.

A STUDY OF NOMINAL INFLECTION IN LATIN INSCRIPTIONS, by Paul A. Gaeng. 1977. (No. 182). -9182-7.

THE LIFE AND WORKS OF LUIS CARLOS LÓPEZ, by Martha S. Bazik. 1977. (No. 183). -9183-5.

"THE CORT D'AMOR". A THIRTEENTH-CENTURY ALLEGORICAL ART OF LOVE, by Lowanne E. Jones. 1977. (No. 185). -9185-1.

PHYTONYMIC DERIVATIONAL SYSTEMS IN THE ROMANCE LANGUAGES: STUDIES IN THEIR ORIGIN AND DEVELOPMENT, by Walter E. Geiger. 1978. (No. 187). -9187-8.

LANGUAGE IN GIOVANNI VERGA'S EARLY NOVELS, by Nicholas Patruno. 1977. (No. 188). -9188-6.

BLAS DE OTERO EN SU POESÍA, by Moraima de Semprún Donahue. 1977. (No. 189). -9189-4.

LA ANATOMÍA DE "EL DIABLO COJUELO": DESLINDES DEL GÉNERO ANATOMÍSTICO, por C. George Peale. 1977. (No. 191). -9191-6.

RICHARD SANS PEUR, EDITED FROM "LE ROMANT DE RICHART" AND FROM GILLES CORROZET'S "RICHART SANS PAOUR", by Denis Joseph Conlon. 1977. (No. 192). -9192-4.

MARCEL PROUST'S GRASSET PROOFS. Commentary and Variants, by Douglas Alden. 1978. (No. 193). -9193-2.

MONTAIGNE AND FEMINISM, by Cecile Insdorf. 1977. (No. 194). -9194-0.

SANTIAGO F. PUGLIA, AN EARLY PHILADELPHIA PROPAGANDIST FOR SPANISH AMERICAN INDEPENDENCE, by Merle S. Simmons. 1977. (No. 195). -9195-9.

BAROQUE FICTION-MAKING. A STUDY OF GOMBERVILLE'S "POLEXANDRE", by Edward Baron Turk. 1978. (No. 196). -9196-7.

THE TRAGIC FALL: DON ÁLVARO DE LUNA AND OTHER FAVORITES IN SPANISH GOLDEN AGE DRAMA, by Raymond R. MacCurdy. 1978. (No. 197). -9197-5.

A BAHIAN HERITAGE. An Ethnolinguistic Study of African Influences on Bahian Portuguese, by William W. Megenney. 1978. (No. 198). -9198-3.

"LA QUERELLE DE LA ROSE: Letters and Documents", by Joseph L. Baird and John R. Kane. 1978. (No. 199). -9199-1.

TWO AGAINST TIME. A Study of the very present worlds of Paul Claudel and Charles Péguy, by Joy Nachod Humes. 1978. (No. 200). -9200-9.

TECHNIQUES OF IRONY IN ANATOLE FRANCE. Essay on Les sept femmes de la Barbe-Bleue, by Diane Wolfe Levy. 1978. (No. 201). -9201-7.

When ordering please cite the ISBN Prefix plus the last four digits for each title.

Send orders to: University of North Carolina Press
Chapel Hill
North Carolina 27514
U. S. A.